Mary Benton was born in Lismore, New South Wales and studied at the University of Sydney and the University of New South Wales. She has worked in a variety of fields including factories, retail, administration and libraries. Her interests include literature, music, theatre, films, philosophy and psychology. She finds politics endlessly fascinating and is a keen follower of current affairs.

She lives in Sydney.

The Goddess Strikes Back

An Autobiography

as narrated to

Mary Benton

First published by MJB Publishing in 2017
This edition published in 2017 by MJB Publishing

Copyright © Mary Benton 2017

The moral right of the author has been asserted.

All rights reserved. This publication (or any part of it) may not be reproduced or transmitted, copied, stored, distributed or otherwise made available by any person or entity (including Google, Amazon or similar organisations), in any form (electronic, digital, optical, mechanical) or by any means (photocopying, recording, scanning or otherwise) without prior written permission from the publisher.

The Goddess Strikes Back

EPUB format: 9781925579321
Print on Demand format: 9781925579338

Cover design by Avril Makula
Image of Bastet, the Cat Goddess of Ancient Egypt, by Gunkarta

Publishing services provided by Critical Mass
www.critmassconsulting.com

Contents

Prologue		1
1.	The Toast of Tibooburra	3
2.	The Early Days	8
3.	The Big Smoke and Beyond	15
4.	Hat	19
5.	Stray Liberation	27
6.	The Roman Connection	32
7.	Down Memory Lane	38
8.	A Bright Young Lawyer	49
9.	The Missing Lynx	54
10.	The Verdict	64
11.	Going Up	68
12.	The Ides of March	74

13.	Hughie Bono	79
14.	Playing Myself	90
15.	The Political Stage	96
16.	The Rigours of Office	103
17.	Bacchus	114
18.	The Ring of Three	125
19.	Breaking the Code	138
20.	The Gold Beetle	150
21.	The Final Stretch	160
22.	The Sting	167

Epilogue	178
Acknowledgements	181

To Veroshka

Prologue

This is it: the autobiography we had to have. Everyone wants to know how I came out of the sticks and nearly took over the whole show. Sit back, relax, and I'll tell you the full story.

Will you hear about my past lives? Of course you will. Time travel is easy. It's like travelling backwards on the XPT, only faster. Thebes, Nineveh, Babylon, Bullamakanka – you name it, I've seen it. And people? I've known just about everybody at one time or another – gods, goddesses, kings, queens, saints, cardinals, explorers, lawyers, politicians – the whole gamut, from the sublime to the ridiculous. Of course I've had to keep the size of the cast down a bit, otherwise we'd end up with *The*

Ten Commandments on our hands. But you will still see plenty. And be warned: I'm not pretending to be perfect. It's a warts and all job.

There are people to thank. Not many, mind you, but I must mention the following. My mother, Colette, without whom, etc.; Matron, a tower of strength; and Queen Hatshepsut of Ancient Egypt, my oldest friend. On the legal side, I must thank Cicero, the master advocate from Ancient Rome, who has been kind enough to keep in touch from time to time, and my local hero, Bob Lyons QC, who gave me a leg-in when no one else wanted to. And a big thank you to Charles Tape and Bill Clayton – what can I say? Thanks also to Ernie Quirk from the Anti-Discrimination Board, to Deirdre Dix, my old sparring partner and campaign manager, to Ted, for all those cups of tea and last but not least, my stenographer Mary Benton.

1

The Toast of Tibooburra

I was born on the wrong side of the Darling. To a lesser talent this would have been fatal, but right from the start I decided to make every post a winner. I'm a survivor.

As you'll discover, my story really starts and finishes with my mother, Colette. She was no ordinary cat. Her origins are a bit mysterious, but they say she was found in a rushwork basket in a Country Women's Association restroom at Tibooburra; a smart Abyssinian wearing an electrum collar engraved simply: *Colette*. Nobody ever turned up to claim her, or the bottle of Bollinger also found in the basket.

Everyone in Tibooburra wanted to adopt her, but she had her own ideas. The Family Hotel was the chosen residence. To this day that bottle of Bollinger has pride of place behind the bar with a sign reading: "Colette Chose The Family Hotel".

On many a sweltering afternoon she'd be seen around the bar exchanging stories with prospectors, hitchhikers, fossil researchers, writers – she could mix it with the best of them. Many a seasoned traveller was stopped in his tracks by a voice from the vicinity of the fridge.

"Welcome to Heartbreak Corner, darling. It's your shout!"

Whereupon she'd leap onto the bar and continue: "Mine's a gin sling – plenty of ice."

The locals loved her. Frankly, she was the toast of the town. She got very friendly with a park ranger who allowed her free access to Sturt National Park. Often she'd be seen around Cameron's Corner, that godforsaken place where the three states meet. There's not much out there: red sand, the dog fence, a white metal post, and a visitors' book. They say I was conceived at Cameron's Corner. For years researchers combed the visitors' book looking for clues, but without success. Colette never went into the details, and I never asked.

Eventually she turned her back on it all – the claypans, the sandhills, the people, the pub – everything she'd known and loved. She headed south to White Cliffs and went underground for a while. Then she moved on to Menindee and from there accompanied some tourists on a one-off trip to Wilcannia by paddle-steamer.

It was love at first sight. At Wilcannia, everything just clicked. The river, the trees, the sandstone buildings, and of course, her new home, St Ives. This was a corrugated-iron establishment situated near Resch's Red Lion Brewery, now the site of the golf club. No one was absolutely sure about its original function, but possession being nine-tenths of the law, it became a refuge for strays way back in the 1880s, in the time of Edward Bulwer Lytton Dickens, the Member for Wilcannia. As to its name, they say it was christened as a joke by EBL himself, after St Ives, a medieval philanthropist and cat lover who, amazingly enough, was the patron saint of lawyers.

In Colette's time St Ives was being looked after by the matron of the local hospital, a cat lover from way back whose faith was being rewarded. She was delighted to discover Colette was extremely talented. They got on famously.

Nothing was too much trouble for Matron. Colette got first choice of everything: food, sleeping arrangements, excursions, books. Matron had been a school teacher before taking up nursing, and they both discovered a common love of the classics, the Latin ones in particular. On Matron's afternoons off they'd walk down to the river, sit under a giant peppercorn tree, and settle into Virgil, Cicero, Horace, or whoever took their fancy that day.

Usually, Ted the postmaster (Matron's fiancé) would bring them down a shandy from the pub. After slaking her thirst Colette was always good for an anecdote or two. One afternoon she surprised Matron by announcing she'd known Julius Caesar when he was in Egypt.

"Were you anyone?" Matron asked.

"I wasn't Cleopatra, if that's what you mean. No, just a bit player, girl about town." Collette sighed. "But I met Caesar. I wish I'd known him better. He was very busy. What with his army occupying Egypt and Cleopatra occupying him, he was flat out. We had a few laughs all the same, and I had a life of my own. Alexandria was the place to be in those days."

"I bet it was. But why did you come back as a cat, and to Australia, of all places?"

Colette considered. "Well there were options. I was on the short list for Number 10 Downing Street at one stage, but was stabbed in the back at the last minute. As a consolation prize I was offered a special assignment in Australia. I accepted. I've always wondered what made the Romans tick, and out here I'm getting a second chance. Now let's get back to Cicero. I love that part where he tears strips off Mark Antony…He's wonderful when he's angry, isn't he?"

Matron blew her nose vigorously and tried to find the page.

2

The Early Days

One night, in the middle of a thunderstorm, Colette gave birth, with Matron in attendance. I was the first out, which I fully expected. At Colette's insistence I was given Matron's name – Mavis – with a Latin chaser: Mavis Augusta in full. I was closely followed by Rex Julius and Joyce Octavia, the latter named after Joyce, the local telephonist, a good friend of Matron's who gave her free calls.

St Ives, though little more than a shed, was an interesting place to live. At night when it rained the noise on the roof was sometimes spooky. Could we hear voices? Ted called the place 'the tin tabernacle'. He told us corrugated iron was

The Goddess Strikes Back

a popular material for building churches in the nineteenth century. It seemed that EBL was on the right track with the name.

Of course we saw a lot of Matron and Ted. Colette used to help out at the post office, cleaning up and providing good entertainment all round. At frequent intervals she would produce a well-pawed Petronius (or some other classic) from under the counter, and give a reading. The author of the week was always written up on the noticeboard behind the cashier. Requests were accepted.

Cicero was the all-time favourite. His murder trials would even draw crowds away from the pub, no mean achievement at forty-five in the shade.

"You are a drink-sodden, sex-ridden wreck!" Colette was shouting from the counter, just as a visiting celebrity walked in. Hot and tired after a day on an outback movie set, our visitor was not impressed. Looking from Colette to Ted he said: "An outback ventriloquist, eh? An unsung Edgar Bergen!"

It took three men to get him off Ted. When he got free, Ted gasped: "It's Colette...she's reading Cicero...he's the author of the week. I'll introduce you."

But Colette had disappeared.

Our visitor was unmoved.

Ted grinned. "It's about Mark Antony."

"He should have sued," the celebrity replied. Thereupon he quickly completed his business and made his exit.

Colette popped up from under the counter. "Antony murdered Cicero, Ted. We were lucky."

The story caught on. From the local paper it made it into one or two of the metropolitan dailies. Years later I met our celebrity's ex-wife. She'd dined out on the story for years.

When Matron and Ted got married we all moved into the postmaster's residence next to the post office. There we started to get an education. I can remember my ears pricking up at the sounds of Seneca when I was still very young.

"She's gifted, Colette," Matron observed.

"Yes, I know. Sometimes I wonder whether I'll be able to cope."

"Of course you will. I'll help. We'll educate them together."

They were keeping up their classical interests and quite a lot rubbed off on us. I suppose it was a bit one-sided, Lucilius and Persius were up and running long before Lawson and Paterson got a guernsey. But where I was going, they were spot on.

Joyce, the telephonist, used to drop in after work for a drink and a talk. She loved a good dose of Juvenal or Petronius. So, along with her own vast experience of local phone conversations, we had some crackerjack evenings.

I progressed so quickly that Colette began to realise Wilcannia wouldn't be big enough to hold me.

"I've got to get some money together," she told Ted and Matron one afternoon in the pub.

"We'll charge admission for your readings," Ted said.

And so, Colette began to earn the money that eventually took us out of Wilcannia and onto the road to fame and fortune. There were other problems, though. Matron was a bit jealous. With a budding genius around there was a subtle shift in the balance of power. She no longer had Colette to herself. Her attempts to discipline me were futile. I know she found Rex and Joyce far more manageable.

"You'll need the patience of a stoic to rear her," she told Colette after some nonsense about a missing budgerigar.

Colette started talking to people around town about places they knew, consulting maps and generally getting her act together. One day she sidled up to a travel-worn hitchhiker who'd walked into the pub. "How many pubs between here and Sydney?" she asked. They had to call in Matron to bring him around.

She saved money religiously and got Ted to place regular bets for her at all the outback race meetings. And when Classical Gas romped home at Birdsville at five hundred to one, she knew she was ready to move.

Ted said: "Look, if you really want to get to the big smoke, I know a bloke in Seven Hills –"

Colette sprang to attention. "What's that?" she asked.

Ted continued: "I know the postmaster at Seven Hills, an outer Sydney suburb."

That was it. How could a lover of all things Roman pass up a place called Seven Hills? And so our giant pub crawl was planned.

I've never forgotten Matron's tear-stained face (whether from joy or sorrow I'm not sure) as we rode away in the back of a Holden station wagon. She and Ted waved for ages until they were just blots on the landscape and then disappeared.

It was a long hard trip to Sydney. We hitchhiked whenever we could. As always the classics were our mainstay, most of the time. I remember one afternoon bumping along a dirt road in the back of a ute, tired and hungry, with Colette reading aloud from Seneca's *Letters from a Stoic* (a farewell gift from Matron).

"It's a rough road that leads to the heights of greatness!" she read.

A split second later there was a big bump, the ute swerved, left the road, and we all ended up in a ditch. Every outback survival kit should leave out *Letters from a Stoic*.

But where Seneca et al really came into their own was as entertainment in the pubs. Colette performed from the classics at every pub we came to. Occasionally there was a feeble attempt at competition from miscellaneous marsupials around the place, but they didn't stand a dog's chance against a real pro. The high point for Colette was the night she played Calpurnia in the Dubbo Dramatic Society's production of *Julius Caesar*. There wasn't a dry eye in the house.

When we finally arrived in Sydney on a grey, wet Sunday afternoon our lift ran out of petrol at the railway workshops at Chullora, and had to let us off there. We were a bit depressed at this stage, so we let our heads go and got a taxi to the RSPCA at Yagoona. Colette thought that after all our scrimping and hitchhiking we deserved to do something in style.

We stayed at the RSPCA overnight, because Colette wanted to be fresh and rested before she met Jim, the postmaster at Seven Hills. Ted had warmly recommended her, and Jim had more or less promised to employ her sight unseen. But she wasn't taking any chances.

"We don't want to look like a bunch of losers," she said.

3

The Big Smoke and Beyond

We settled in very quickly at Seven Hills. Jim turned out to be a pushover, so we had the run of the place in no time. Colette was busy working at the post office and giving us an education. We got a thorough grounding in the three Rs – racing, ratting, and resting – but she also believed in the artistic options, like reading, writing, and arithmetic.

Rex, who loved performing, started working in commercials early on, and later became a minor celebrity in his own right. Octavia (she'd decided to drop Joyce) was a pretty little thing, and started to get a lot of card and calendar work. As for myself, being the intellectual heavyweight of the three, I stuck to the classics and philosophy. In the little matter of my name, I decided to opt for the lesser of two evils and tough it out with Mavis.

Much to Colette's delight I joined her in a double act. We developed a very big following with the weekly event *Classics at the Post Office*, in which we read from the classics to a packed house. Inner-city intellectuals would get into traffic jams every Friday night, just to squeeze into Seven Hills Post Office and rub shoulders with the Westies. It was amazing.

All in all, those early days at Seven Hills were very happy. And just as well, because what eventuated a little later really shook us up. Colette had decided I should get my Higher School Certifcate and with Jim's help, hired a special tutor for the purpose, a clever young man from the Anti-Discrimination Board named Ernie Quirk.

Not only was Ernie a super teacher but he also handled all the red tape for my application to sit for the examinations. I think the powers that be decided they may as well humour us.

The fun started when the results came out. I'd topped the state in Latin. And the fact that Ernie's auntie was a tea lady in the Examinations Board had nothing to do with it. It was my first brush with the tall poppy syndrome. Horace was so right when he said: "It's the tall poppy that the lightning strikes." The resulting furore broke Colette's heart and Ernie's bank balance, and even though we won the court case I was shattered.

I had intended to go straight on to university, but I just didn't have the heart. The only positive thing to come out of it was my realising that, failing a Lotto win, a legal career would make a good second choice. But I was too upset to think about anything clearly. In fact I just ran off, leaving a quick goodbye note and promising to be in touch soon.

I headed north, hitchhiking all the way. There were plenty of people willing to give me a lift, and meals were easy to come by. With all the publicity I'd had, lots of people recognised me.

"Good on you, Mave," they'd say. "Come and stay the night."

I met some beautiful people this way. I'd stay for a couple of days then move on, sometimes leaving a little message in a note. The friends I made during this period never forgot me. Much later, so many of them helped in my political campaign in rural seats. And today those notes fetch a small fortune at auction.

I travelled on through Ballina, Byron Bay, Brunswick Heads, following the great caravan trails of the north, trying to forget Sydney and the whole mess. I really wanted to get myself together. For a while I sat at the feet of the northern visionary, Hildegard of Nimbin, and we mulled over the mushrooms. But ultimately I moved on, still feeling unsatisfied.

Finally, I settled at Fingal, a small village south of Tweed Heads. I made friends, rested, went fishing, and started to enjoy life again. Things went fairly quietly for a while. Then it happened.

4

Hat

I was having dinner with friends in Fingal's Steak Cave, an atmospheric little restaurant perched on Fingal Head, overlooking the ocean. After a couple of pinot noirs I repaired to the verandah for a breather. Looking down at the breakers pounding onto the rocks I felt a bit dizzy. The wind roared, the gulls screeched. There was a whirring sound, my surroundings seemed to recede, then everything went black. It was my first XPT experience.

I awoke to find myself on a boat on a river under an electric blue sky. I looked about me. To the left was a teeming metropolis. Craft of all descriptions were moored to the quayside.

Beyond these were warehouses and mud brick dwellings of all shapes and sizes. Further back were grander houses and temples. Magnificent pylons and obelisks thrust into the sky. Memories came flooding back. This was Thebes on the Nile. To the right was a ridge of brown cliffs cracked and parched in the sun. My observations were interrupted.

"Well, look who's here!" I was being addressed by a slim, attractive woman in her early thirties. I immediately recognised my old friend Queen Hatshepsut of the Eighteenth Dynasty, the first woman to rule Egypt.

"Hat!" I exclaimed.

"Mavis!"

"How long's it been?" I asked.

"Oh, about three and a half thousand years," she replied.

"You don't look a day over a hundred and fifty, darling."

"Who's counting?" she said. "And you haven't changed a bit."

"When you're on a good thing, stick to it," I said.

The great thing about old friends is it doesn't matter how long it's been since you've seen them. You just take up where you left off.

The Goddess Strikes Back

"How's the family?" I asked.

Hat wasn't amused. As half of them were trying to do her in, I suppose it wasn't surprising.

"Never mind about that," she replied. "We're here to talk about you."

Uh-oh, I thought. Here we go again.

Just to stall things a bit I asked: "How's the Funerary Temple going?"

"It's finished. I'll show you." With that she ordered the steersman to head for shore.

Upon disembarking we boarded a waiting litter.

"Deir-el-Bahri, driver!" Hat commanded. "On the double!"

We talked as we rode.

"I think you'll be impressed," Hat said.

I could tell she was thrilled to bits. The temple had been designed by Senmut, her chief architect, and constant companion.

"Where's Sen, anyway?" I asked.

"He's away on business."

"That's what they all say."

As we approached our destination, I was overwhelmed. Cut into rock at the bottom of giant cliffs was a vast temple in shades of golden-white limestone. We alighted from the litter and proceeded on foot. Stretching before us were two magnificent terraces planted with myrrh trees. Cutting through the terraces was an avenue lined with pink granite sphinxes in Hat's likeness.

As we walked up the first avenue I said: "It's almost worth dying for, Hat."

"Almost," she agreed.

We entered a courtyard planted with young vines and palm trees. Hat paused to inspect them.

"They're coming along quite nicely," she said.

We continued on through the second terrace that led us to a great columned portico. Upon entering we were confronted with a series of colossal statues of Hat in the likeness of Osiris, the god of the Underworld.

I was floored. "How many statues are there?" I asked as we wove our way through them like pygmies walking between lines of giants.

"Twenty-six," she replied.

"You haven't got one too many?" I quipped.

She flicked me on the ear and laughed.

Beyond that portico I could see a great pillared hall in shades of pink and buff.

"What's in there?" I asked.

"The sanctuaries and the inner sanctum itself – the Royal Funerary Chapel. I'd like Senmut to show you all that."

"I'd love to see it," I said.

"Not just now, Mavis. How about some dinner back at the palace?"

I didn't argue. I was hungry and looking forward to a meal.

"Take my advice," Hat said as we walked. "Get your act together and go back to Sydney. You'll never get anywhere bumming around the North Coast. I didn't get where I am swanning around Thebes and Karnak. I worked for it."

As we entered the palace Hat indicated to her retinue she didn't want to be disturbed. We swept through lavishly decorated halls, luxuriously draped and furnished rooms, past columns inlaid with gold and exquisite enamel panelling. Many walls and ceilings were colourfully painted depicting family gatherings and historical scenes decorated with flowers, birds and wildlife of all descriptions. Then there came my favourite floor – a painted lagoon full of fish and carpeted with waterlilies.

"Come on Mavis, it's only a painting," Hat called as I dallied.

We walked through a corridor of polished bronze mirrors and nearly collided. Shaken by this, we were pleased to be ushered into Hat's private apartments. She kicked off her sandals and relaxed into her favourite chair. I ran underneath it and settled down. Just like old times.

"Come out of there, I want to talk to you," she said.

I didn't budge. I hadn't come back three and a half thousand years just to get a lecture.

"Come on," she said coaxingly.

I was determined not to come out. She bent down to look at me under the chair. As she did so her wig fell askew.

"You'd better call the hairdresser," I observed. And just to make myself perfectly clear I pulled a thread on her linen shift. She rose and tried to kick me, catching her shin on the chair as she did so.

"Blast!" she hissed, and yelled for her lady-in-waiting, who helped her adjust her wig and took her order for dinner.

I decided to make myself scarce.

We made peace with each other over a lovely meal: bread, lentil soup, roast gazelle, and cucumber salad. We consumed a couple of jugs of beer as well. To finish off, we picked from two huge bowls of grapes and figs.

Hat called for more beer.

"I'll bring you some Resch's next time," I said.

"You're on," she replied.

We were both feeling mellow by this time.

Hat spoke: "I was so upset when you died."

"So was I," I replied.

"I wept and wailed, shaved my eyebrows, and went into mourning for six months."

"I was watching. You looked ridiculous, you really did."

I'd been accidentally killed by a throwing stick (a sort of Egyptian boomerang) on a hunting trip with Hat. An inept attendant had managed to hit me instead of the duck.

"It was such a silly way to go, Mavis."

"Don't rub it in," I replied.

"I had the fool executed, of course."

"I've come back now, just like a boomerang. So you'd better watch out."

After a few minutes of reverie she said: "Look, I think your morale needs a boost. They're having a sale in Bubastis tomorrow. Bastet, the cat goddess, is getting rid of her old clothes. It's all up for grabs. I think you should go and get yourself an outfit. You have to look the part to get on in Sydney."

The next day I got a fast barge up to Bubastis to be at the sale when the doors opened. It was a knockout. First in, best dressed. When I stepped back into Fingal's Steak Cave I'd been transformed.

I wore a lovely striped frock, gold earrings in pierced ears, and a cowrie shell necklace. This latter was pure Fingal. To top it off, I carried a big rushwork basket with lots of interesting trinkets inside.

My friends were worried. "Where were you? Your steak's cold. We're on to coffee and liqueurs."

"Oh, I just ran into an old mate on the verandah. We got talking and she sold me an outfit."

Over Campari I told them my days on the coast were numbered, and I'd be going back to Sydney. The next morning I rang Colette, booked a sleeper and started packing.

5

Stray Liberation

As the train pulled in to Central I looked out the window and saw the old familiar face there to greet me. Colette was jubilant as I stepped off the train.

"I'd scarcely have known you," she said, admiring my new outfit. "And where did you get those earrings?"

"I picked them up at a little place on the river," I replied.

We chatted as we waited for a taxi. Since I'd left town everyone had been going places. Jim had helped Colette form her own pest control outfit, the Necessary Cat Company, and she'd moved from Seven Hills to Alexandria.

Octavia had gone into modelling in a big way, getting a foot into the international market. And Rex had made a name for himself as a TV performer and was being groomed for stardom by the famous acting coach Felix Friend. I could see I'd have to get moving.

That afternoon I went to see Ernie Quirk. He was really pleased to see me.

"Ernie, I want to be a fat cat," I said.

"You are already, aren't you?"

"Now don't get funny, Ernie. I want to be a lawyer. I want to be a top silk."

"That's great. We'll have to get you into university. No problems. I'll sort it out for you."

And so I started an arts/law degree at Sydney University. How well I remember orientation week. I was courted by every club and society going, from the Rock Climbers to the Libertarians. I had a lot in common with both of these, but ambitious people have to set their priorities early. You only have so much time. Some groups were anathema, of course. I remember passing the Rodents' Rights stall and shivering all over. But then I found it – a stall with a large banner reading: "Stray Liberation Movement". In small print there was more: "Bring strays in from the cold; end discrimination; provide housing, food, sickness benefits, workers' compensation, educational opportunities" etc.

I knew I'd come to the right place. I joined up on the spot. As it happened, the president of the movement was there at the time: a spiky-haired lady named Deirdre Dix. A vision in battle fatigues. Deirdre was a political science student with an eye on the wider arena. We hit it off immediately.

If I hadn't been so determined on a legal career I might have been tempted to major in classics, but I did keep going with Latin anyway. I was popular on campus. At first I was a bit of a novelty, but when people realised I was a serious student things settled down.

I organised my time well, kept up with my studies but also indulged in extracurricular activities. I was living with Colette at Alexandria at the time. Stray Liberation was a popular movement, with lots of meetings and activities. Deirdre maintained that ultimately the movement would have to spread out from campus and encompass the whole community.

I got to know Deirdre pretty well as time went on. One night over coffee at Manning she told me her life story. Tragic.

"It's a hard world, Mavis," she said. "That's why we've got to change it."

"Starting with the strays," I said.

"That's right."

"Colette's made a start with the Necessary Cat Company."

"A capitalist cop-out!" she spat.

"Well, it's a start."

I didn't really see eye to eye with Deirdre on everything, but I felt it might be worthwhile sticking with her for the time being. She had a talent for management and lots of contacts. We decided to rent a flat together and put an ad in the newspapers:

WANTED, SUNNY FLAT FOR IDEOLOGICALLY SOUND LADY AND BRILLIANT COMPANION. CLOSE COCKROACHES, MICE, CHEAP EATS.

In no time we got a lovely little place at Darling Street, Rozelle. We were good for each other, and we both did well in our end-of-year exams.

During my second year at uni things really started to happen. The movement was spreading beyond campus. Deirdre had put in a lot of work. Territory was being established. A force could be felt moving through the inner city suburbs and beyond: Chippendale, Redfern, Surry Hills, Darlinghurst, Kings Cross, Woolloomooloo, Ultimo, Pyrmont, Balmain. Branches sprang up in all of them. Several State MPs had been approached and a draft bill was being prepared.

Our dreams came true at the opening of the Darling Point branch. Amid the champagne and caviar the Premier and his wife dropped in. He promised us he'd get the legislation through parliament. After he left I was the toast of the branch.

"Without you no one would have taken any notice," they said.

Deirdre was jubilant and in her enthusiasm hired a white Mercedes. We sped through the city visiting other branches and telling them the good news. I felt so happy I wondered if politics rather than the law should be my ultimate goal.

As if reading my thoughts Deirdre remarked: "We'd make a great team."

6

The Roman Connection

The climax came when the Premier invited Deirdre and me to a party at his house at Darling Point. It was a wonderful evening. Everybody who was anybody was there. To cap it all we were told the Stray Liberation Bill was a cinch.

I roamed around a bit, just to get the feel of the place. Then it happened. The oldest story in the book. A look across a crowded patio and my world changed. The earth moved, skyrockets blazed into the night sky, and I was in love. His name was Cicero. A black and white god. He was silver-tongued and silver-tailed.

What a night! I don't know what happened to Deirdre except that she went home early.

The Goddess Strikes Back

Cicero and I went out to see the sights of Darling Point, arriving back at dawn.

"Why don't you stay for breakfast?" suggested Cicero. "The old man (meaning the Premier) won't mind. My word's law around here anyway."

How could I resist? As a matter of fact I stayed on for two days, until Deidre showed up looking very put out.

"Don't you remember," she accused, "we promised to go and see your mother today."

"Okay, okay," I said.

I said goodbye to Cicero and off we drove to Alexandria. On the way we had a blazing row. Deirdre was in her separatist phase at that stage and thought my affair with Cicero was ridiculous.

"You're turning into a doormat," she fumed. "Over there at his beck and call. It'll ruin your looks, your talent, your career..."

"It's only been thirty-six hours," I replied.

She wasn't to be deterred. "You'll turn into a fat, boring, suburban nobody!"

This was too much. I took a swipe at her left ear. Suddenly a semitrailer was coming straight for us. We swerved – just in time – and pulled in to the curb.

"Look," I said, as we caught our breath, "we'll *both* end up as doormats if we keep this up."

We agreed on a truce for the rest of the drive.

Colette was delighted when I told her about my friend at the Premier's place.

"What a catch," she breathed, "living in luxury at Darling Point, privy to power and patronage. Darling, this could be a very important connection. What's his name?"

"Cicero."

Colette went into a swoon and had to lie down. I noticed a gin bottle lying in the corner.

"Colette, you haven't been drinking again, have you?"

She ignored this and continued: "Mavis, this will be a meaningful relationship. It's the Roman connection...at last. Cicero communicating with us from the past...I think he's trying to come through now."

She touched her temples and seemed to go into a kind of trance. I was worried. She murmured something I couldn't make out, then lapsed into Latin.

"*Arma virumque cano*," she intoned.

"Oh my God," I gasped.

"What is she saying?" Deirdre asked.

"It's the opening line of the *Aeneid*," I replied.

"The *Aeneid*!" she exclaimed. "But Virgil wrote that, didn't he?"

The Goddess Strikes Back

"That's what worries me," I said. "I thought Cicero was on the line."

Colette droned on with bits and pieces from the classics – Virgil, Cicero, Horace. Sometimes it was gibberish. Suddenly there was a loud rapping noise.

Deirdre went pale and sank into a chair. "There *is* a spirit here," she whispered.

"Oh, for heaven's sake, get hold of yourself," I snapped. Then more gently: "There's someone knocking at the door. Go and answer it, there's a good girl."

Colette had gone very quiet. I grabbed a sprig of catnip and waved it under her nose. This brought her around a bit. She opened her eyes.

I said quietly: "Look darling, we don't want to rush Cicero, do we? Let's take it one step at a time. Let's stay cool."

"All right, dear. I'll try to be sensible."

Deirdre returned with a funny look on her face. She was carrying a small parcel.

"Who was it?" I asked.

"There was no one there," she said, "but this parcel was outside the door...the greeting card reads: *To Colette, with love from Virgil.*"

I turned to Colette: "Who's Virgil?" I asked sharply.

"Never you mind," she replied, looking very pleased with herself.

And that was all she'd say.

The months went by. I saw Cicero and the Premier as often as I could. In fact, I moved into the house at Darling Point permanently. The Premier was very tolerant. Deirdre accused me of being an elitist.

"All right, I'm an elitist doormat. So what?" I said.

I was having a great social life through being based at Darling Point. I met everybody. It was a wonderful period while it lasted. Colette was very interested in all my doings and visited often. That's how I eventually met Virgil, a marmalade charmer who was co-managing the Necessary Cat Company with her. I was pleased she'd found someone. After all, she wasn't getting any younger. She invited us round to Alexandria quite often. We made a great foursome. The social pages dubbed us "The Alexandria Quartet".

Colette told me Cicero was too good to pass up.

"You should make it a permanent commitment," she said.

"Don't push it," was all I'd say.

But she wasn't to be deterred. I was alarmed one day when a beautifully wrapped parcel arrived at Darling Point. The tag was ominous. It read: *To Cicero, with love from Colette*. Inside was an exquisite gold canary inscribed: "The virtue of parents is a great dowry – Horace".

Luckily Cicero wasn't around at the time and I got to the parcel first. I hid the canary immediately. But something had taken root in my mind. Maybe she had the right idea. And very slowly and subtly I began thinking "this is for keeps".

What a fool I was! I won't bore you with all the details: the faraway look in the eye, the silences, the unexplained absences, the neglect, the hurt. So I won't. But that should give you a bit of an idea. I could reel off a string of names too: Minette de Coeur, Selima Smart, Koshka Conway. But I won't. I'll just name those three.

And to cap everything, we had a political disaster. An Independent switched sides at the last minute and the Stray Liberation Bill was defeated. I was devastated and went into a clinic for a minor operation that was the subject of a lot of unnecessary speculation.

As a matter of fact I remember very little of that period, except for my trip back to Hat. I stayed a fortnight. Unfortunately, I forgot the Resch's.

7

Down Memory Lane

There I was, back at Thebes again. I gazed across the green expanse of the Nile to those ancient brown cliffs and the funerary temples. That's where we all ended up in the finish – in a tomb.

Oh, what was the point of it all? Try as I might I couldn't get rid of my depression. I walked, I prayed, I ate, I drank, I languished under date palms. To no avail.

Seeing I was in a bad way Hat insisted I accompany her everywhere. I sat in on talks with her priests and advisers; went to banquets; travelled on the Royal Barge; walked through orchards; went on hunting, shooting and fishing trips; stayed in her private rooms overnight. I had

The Goddess Strikes Back

everything a person in old Egypt could wish for. But there was a worm at the heart of things.

One day I looked over the interior of Hat's Funerary Chapel with Senmut. He explained the whole layout to me: how he would be buried there too, secretly, so they'd be together for eternity. I thought of myself: where will I be buried? Who have I got lined up for eternity? Nobody. I couldn't even manage three months at Darling Point!

Inconsolable, I hid for days in a papyrus thicket near the palace. Hat and Sen finally found me and hauled me out. That night, over roast duck and date pudding they tried to talk sense into me. But I wouldn't come round.

Hat cleared her throat. "I think this calls for special measures," she said. She looked at Sen and nodded. Then she continued: "I want to make a phone call…in private."

"Come on, Mavis." I followed Sen to the door, and just managed to catch Hat's first words as she picked up the receiver.

"Hello, operator…get me Bubastis One, please. Person to person."

Next day Hat and Sen ushered me into a plush theatrette, complete with projector and movie screen.

"Do you like it?" Hat asked.

"Terrific!" I exclaimed.

Sen spoke: "I designed the theatre and Sam Goldwyn gave us the movie equipment. A great friend."

I was dazzled.

"Sen, will you run it for us?" Hat asked, handing him a reel of film.

"What's all this about?" I asked.

"The cat goddess thinks you need cheering up."

We sank into red velvet armchairs and made ourselves comfortable. Sen was up the back fiddling with the projector.

As the lights dimmed I heard a rustling noise from Hat's direction. Irritated, I looked across and saw her opening a box of Fantales.

"I'll have one of those, thank you," I said.

The screen flickered and a clapperboard appeared reading: *MAVIS – LIVES*.

Then things started to roll.

The first picture showed a fuzzy close-up of a lion's head. For a moment I thought MGM was in on the act. No such luck. A caption read: *The Subject Was Noses*.

"Noses?" I exclaimed.

The focus cleared. All I could see was a scraggy mane and an enormous nose.

"You were a lion in one life," Hat said.

"So I see...God, I'm thin, and look at that nose, it's huge!"

Hat chuckled. "Yes, it is big, isn't it? Cyrano de Bergerac eat your heart out!"

I was really nettled.

As the film continued the lion ambled about some studio jungle. I exploded.

"This isn't cheering me up. It's boring. We need a new director, Hat!"

"Life with the lions is a bit dull, eh? Okay, let's move on. Sen!"

The screen blurred. Then came a caption reading: *The One that Got Away: Fishing with Her Favourite Pharaohs – Medley.* I immediately sparked up. A fishing trip on the Nile on a good day – nothing like it.

After the spectacle Hat asked: "Feeling more cheerful?"

"Much."

"What about the one that got away?"

"Who cares! You win some, you lose some!"

Now we were in different territory altogether: *The Avengers: Alexandria, 48 BC.*

A cat is sitting on a doorstep minding her own business.

"That's you," Hat said.

A Roman soldier lurches into the picture. Obviously drunk, he trips and falls on top of the cat. Blackness. I watched the screen, riveted.

'What's up, Sen?" I shouted. "Has the projector conked out, or what?"

The next frame told the story. The cat is dead and the soldier is dead drunk beside her. A crowd of Egyptians is forming, and they are angry.

Someone shouts: "He's killed a sacred animal. Get him! Kill him!"

They made short work of him. Tore him to shreds.

I spoke. "He had that coming, the idiot. I was having a great time in Alexandria. Wait till I tell Colette. She thinks the Romans are all cute and clever like Caesar and Cicero."

On we moved. The next caption read: *Sweet Charity: Brittany, 1300. Saint Ives Visits a Client.*

A man in medieval robes is talking to a man lying in bed. A cat sits on the end of the bed.

Hat said: "That's you and St Ives on hospital rounds."

"I knew St Ives would be in the act somewhere," I replied. "Who's the man in the bed?"

"Watch," Hat said.

The Goddess Strikes Back

St Ives is serving a bowl of soup to the man, who eats it hungrily. St Ives and the cat prepare to leave.

The man speaks: "How can I ever repay you? You've been my advocate in court, and you still haven't sent the bill. You've fed and looked after me here. I owe you so much."

St Ives smiled. "There's no need to repay me."

As he and the cat approach the door, the cat looks back and speaks: "One day you'll be the Member for Wilcannia – name a building after him."

Fade.

"So EBL came through," I said.

"He didn't hurt himself," Hat replied.

"St Ives – the Poor Man's Lawyer. He didn't have a dime, the silly blighter. God, some people will do anything to get canonised."

"You heartless little sod," Hat said. "I wasn't going to run the witch hunts with all the torturing of cats, but you need a lesson –"

"Oh no, not the witch hunts. No Hat, please!" I shrieked. "Please, Sen," I whimpered.

"All right, then. But brush up."

The next caption was intriguing: *Witness for the Prosecution: The Queen of Hampton Court Visits the Star Chamber.*

Cardinal Wolsey, a massively built man of great presence, is sitting with the Council of the Star Chamber. He is personally questioning a defendant who is on his knees begging for mercy. A grand-looking cat sits impassively by the cardinal, staring at the defendant with unblinking eyes. The man is howling and grovelling.

The cat looks at Wolsey and speaks. "Come on Tom, I'm hungry. Send him to the Tower, and let's get back to Hampton Court."

Fade.

My pulse was racing. "Oh, I miss Hampton Court – rolling hills, lawns, parks, game. And being with Wolsey – that was power!"

"You haven't improved much," Hat said.

I called out: "Sen, have you got anything with hearts in it? Hat's getting worried."

Suddenly the voltage dropped dramatically: *Kind Hearts and Coronets,* the caption read. We're knee deep in Victoriana: velvet cushions, satin ribbons, hearth, home, and heaven knows what. I'm reclining beside Queen Victoria posing for a family photograph. A coronet is sitting uneasily over my ears. All the family is assembled.

"Oh god," I groaned, "this will take hours. White Heather was her favourite cat anyway… and that coronet gave me dermatitis."

The Goddess Strikes Back

"Okay, we'll move on," Hat said. "Fade it, Sen," she called.

"And now for something completely different," Hat announced. "The Australian outback."

I waited eagerly.

The caption appears: *The Lady Vanishes Or the Mother of Australian Exploration*. My ears pricked up.

Hat was rattling some papyrus sheets. "I've got a bit of commentary to do here," she said.

She cleared her throat and began to read: "Dusk descends on Fort Grey in northwestern New South Wales. Captain Charles Sturt and his men are returning from the Dead Heart. They are scurvy-ridden and exhausted."

We see a bedraggled group of men sitting by a camp fire cooking a meal. A caption reads: *There was no inland sea*.

Hat exclaimed: "This is awful. We'll have to cheer them up."

The dusk deepens. A full moon hangs over the scene. From the dried out bed of Lake Pinaroo a figure emerges. She is wearing a striped gown, and carrying a rushwork basket over one arm. She enters the camp and from the basket passes round limes to the men. They are jubilant. She gets three cheers.

Hat read on: "Thanks to our friend, Sturt rallied enough to take his last desperate non-stop ride to Depot Glen, sixty-two miles to the south, where he found water."

Hat then read from a lost fragment of Sturt's journal: "A most superior lady of unusual talents joined the party at Fort Grey, and remained with us as far as Menindee. Not only providing desperately needed lime juice and a shower of rain, but giving such grand companionship all round that our spirits rose dramatically. She charmed the dogs, caught plenty of fowl, and gave much laughter and entertainment to the whole party. I pressed upon her my wish that she accompany us back to Adelaide but, one night, at Menindee Lakes, as abruptly as she first appeared, she vanished.

"You're a bloody marvel," Hat observed.

I was quite overcome. "There should be a monument out there in the Sturt National Park. A sculpture in granite: 'The Mother of Australian Exploration'."

"You want to follow that up when you get back," Hat replied.

"It would leave that dog on the tuckerbox for dead!" I exclaimed.

The screen faded.

"And now for a big finish," Hat said.

The Goddess Strikes Back

The caption reads: *A Star Is Born*.

On the screen there is a vast desert, as far as the eye can see. A tiny spot appears on the tip of the horizon. Ever so slowly the spot grows bigger and appears to be coming closer.

"How about the soundtrack, Sen?" Hat called.

Soft drumbeat is heard. Then a tune I can't quite make out, in a halting rhythm. It is maddeningly familiar – variations on something. The spot on the screen is coming closer – I can just make out a figure on horseback, in flowing robes...Arab dress...The strings become more assertive – a vast flowing melody is lifting –

"Lawrence of Arabia!" I shouted.

At his side he's clutching something...it looks like me.

"Oh, I don't believe it," I said, and broke up.

Hat spoke: "He rescued you when you fell behind. You were his mascot. You helped him in all his campaigns. The unsung heroine of the Arab Revolt – Mavis of Mesopotamia!"

"The Tigress of the Euphrates!" Sen exclaimed as he joined us. "Well, Mavis, the show's over. How do you feel?"

"I feel like a Resch's," I replied.

"Can't oblige with a Resch's, but we've got some home brew."

Mary Benton

Sen poured us all a beer.
"Here's to past lives," he said.
"And to the future," I replied.

8

A Bright Young Lawyer

I got back to Sydney in a big hurry. Devouring the rest of my course in short order, I picked up a First in Latin and went on to get the University Medal in Law. I also picked up the gold canary on one late-night visit to Darling Point.

Colette was very proud of me. She was doing well too. The Necessary Cat Company was expanding rapidly under her watchful eye, and branches appeared in many suburbs. The high point was the opening of a branch in St Ives, a posh suburb on Sydney's north side. Virgil was a tower of strength, but Cicero was never mentioned. He could fritter his life away in Darling Point if he wanted to. We had bigger fish to fry.

Deirdre graduated at the same time as I did and stayed on with the Stray Liberation Movement as a full-time administrator. She alleviated times of negative cash flow (one of her favourite phases) with stints of investigative journalism. She wanted me to stay in the movement, but the Bar was calling.

I had decided I wanted to be admitted straight away. Why fiddle around on the sidelines if you want to get into the big league? I experienced a bit of opposition. It was one thing for me to be picking up gold medals in the groves of academe, but wanting to mix it with the big boys in chambers was a different ball game altogether. In the legal fraternity there were roughly two schools of thought about me. To one camp I was the greatest thing since the talkies. To the other I heralded the end of civilisation as we know it.

Luckily reason prevailed, and I was duly admitted. It was a great day. Matron and Ted came down from Wilcannia. Jim came in from Seven Hills. Rex and Octavia flew in from LA, and of course there were Colette and Virgil. I even got a phone call from the Premier.

I was accepted into chambers as a pupil of Bob Lyons, a well-known QC. Reading in Chambers, they call it. I had a great time. Bob and I got on splendidly and we were on first name terms straight away. He showed me everything. I read his briefs, visited the library, sat in on consultations with his clients. Bob found the latter practice much to his liking.

"You have a calming affect on them," he said. "Sitting there in the corner of the room you give them a sense of security." Bob was warming to his theme. He continued: "You represent stability, hearth and home – a benign presence assuring them that order and right values will prevail."

"Yes, Bob," I said simply, wondering if he had the right person.

Accompanying Bob to court was the best part. Sitting behind him, listening to the cut and thrust of the courtroom drama, I knew I was in the right place.

I was a bit of a sensation around Phillip Street for a while. Crowds would gather as Bob, his associates, and I strode from his chambers to the Supreme Court, wigs in place, gowns flying. I became a regular tourist attraction. The Opera House, Mrs Macquarie's Chair, Centrepoint Tower, and me crossing Phillip Street became a very popular package tour. So many people wanted to sit in on cases that Bob had the Banco Court permanently booked.

Eventually things settled down as the novelty wore off. In due course I had a few little cases thrown my way, leftovers mostly. A Rodents' Rights brief I found particularly trying. But Bob explained that a good advocate must always put aside his personal bias.

Slowly I began to establish my own practice. Once people realised I was able to do the job, they stopped worrying. A very satisfactory early victory was one involving the Stray Liberation Movement. I won the case easily. Deirdre was jubilant.

I quickly found my feet after that. I was a very tough barrister. Careful preparation was my hallmark. My questioning usually began slowly, even playfully. Witnesses were lulled into a false sense of security before I struck. My unblinking stare combined with suddenness and sureness of attack were a fatal combination. Witnesses would break down and confess in the witness stand, and have to be helped from the court by paramedics. Not since the days of Perry Mason had such devastation been seen in a courtroom. Artists' impressions of some of these encounters are now collectors' items.

My reputation was building nicely. Then came a somewhat unusual case. It became known as the Missing Lynx Scandal. What a case it was. Talk about bread and circuses! It was the turning point of my career.

9

The Missing Lynx

This was the story. Claude Bell, an eastern suburbs playboy and hell-raiser, had gatecrashed a "women only" consciousness-raising meeting at the Double Bay home of Polly King, estranged wife of Jerry King, a well-known figure in state politics. I'd known them both in my Darling Point days. Polly was keen on women's issues and wanted to start a lobby group.

Bell, expertly made up (including a puttied nose) and wearing glasses, wig, and full female regalia, had succeeded in gaining entrance to the meeting. It was a large and diverse group of women, including quite a few visitors from out of town. Dress ranged from Polly's silk frock down to designer overalls worn by my old friend Deirdre Dix. An object of general admiration was a brand-new lynx fur coat, worn by Vera Stone-Marten, a well-heeled socialite and friend of Polly's. Currently between divorces, Vera had decided to test the waters of feminism. Bell was allegedly in the casual employ of *SPIV*, a girlie magazine with intellectual pretensions. The object being an exposé, from the male point of view, of what went on at the meeting.

Bell played his part to the hilt, mixing well with participants who, thinking the lady slightly odd, didn't twig to the truth. He even went to the lengths of admiring and talking to the babies who had been brought along with their mothers. Only once did he overdo it by speaking baby talk to a securely wrapped bundle in a pram, which turned out to be a well-chilled wine cask and not a baby at all.

The first half of the evening involved a general meeting and discussion. There was a break for supper to be followed by a series of role-playing exercises to be performed then discussed by the group.

During the supper break, while drinks were liberally imbibed from a large Wedgwood punchbowl, Bell and Vera had a long tête-à-tête and became quite chummy. She even allowed him to try on her fur coat. He was still wearing it when Polly called everyone together and asked for two volunteers for the first role play. Vera and Bell volunteered immediately and ascended the podium. Bell (still wearing the coat) played an inconsiderate, irate husband, and Vera a wife on the defensive but trying to be assertive.

It was obvious Bell had had a few drinks, and he played the role with gusto. But as the performance proceeded he became visibly hostile. Vera in turn became angry and rattled.

"You're an unfaithful, nagging, money hungry bitch!" he shouted.

"You're a womanising, lying skinflint!"

The audience was becoming restive.

"Don't overdo it. We are trying to be constructive," someone said.

Bell was undeterred. "Like all women you're unreliable, masochistic and stupid!"

"Don't talk to me like that! Who do you think you are, anyway?"

The tension was broken by the phone ringing. Polly answered it on a nearby extension. After talking briefly Polly looked towards the tableau.

"It's for you, Vera," she said.

The Goddess Strikes Back

Vera stepped off the podium and went to the phone. Everyone watched and waited as if for a sign. As she listened to whoever was calling her expression hardened and her eyes gleamed. She said a few words then hung up. She strode back to her position on centre stage and looked triumphantly at the audience.

"Ladies," she said slowly, "there's been some very disturbing news. That was a journalist friend on the phone. There is an imposter in the room." She looked towards Bell. "A man in drag, working for a girlie magazine, is here to spy on us."

The room was abuzz. Each woman looked at the one next to her.

Vera confronted Bell. "Who are you?" she asked. "And take that coat off."

The question was echoed by the audience.

"Yes, who are you?" we heard from various points in the room.

Bell looked nervous. "I've already said who I am…I'm…Penelope Weaver…a deserted wife trying to make a fresh start –"

Vera cut in: "You told me your name was Troy, Helen Troy. I thought that sounded odd."

"Helen's my second name – Troy was my maiden name."

"Maiden, my foot!" shouted Deirdre Dix.

"Helen Troy – just back from Paris, eh? Why you phoney!" said Vera.

Bell said: "Look, I'm sorry everyone. I have to go to the bathroom."

He left the room hurriedly, heading straight for the back of the house, and went out towards the area beside the swimming pool. Vera and Deirdre were in hot pursuit.

"That's not the way to the bathroom!" Vera shouted. "And take off that coat!"

They tried to intercept him. There was a scuffle.

"You're an imposter!" cried Deirdre, pulling at his wig. Vera made a grab for the coat, but he pushed her aside. Another woman, an investigative journalist named Sara Blunt, joined the confrontation.

"I think I know who you are," she said. "Take those glasses off."

What happened beside the pool after that depends on who's telling the story. But an eyewitness later confirmed that a figure wearing a fur coat was seen running down New South Head Road at great speed. At some stage during the sprint the culprit dispensed with the coat, jumped a fence and disappeared into somebody's garden. At that point a passing car slowed down and stopped. An occupant alighted, picked up the coat, returned to the car, and sped off. Vera and Deirdre then appeared on the scene, but too late. But not too late to get the make and number of the vehicle. Out of breath and disconsolate, they returned to the house.

Sara was lying beside the pool, unconscious. Doctor, police, and ambulance were called. Statements were taken. Vera and Deirdre, the only witnesses to the scuffle beside the pool, were adamant that the assailant had struck and pushed Sara who then fell and hit her head. They were certain of his identity – Claude Bell – and denied any provocation for the action.

Investigations continued, but Bell couldn't be found. None of his friends or associates seemed to know where he was. Gone to the country, some thought. Forensic evidence was collected. The remaining contents of the punch bowl was found to contain a significant amount of ecstasy – a drug all the rage in the eastern suburbs at the time.

All participants denied any knowledge of the drug, as *SPIV* magazine denied all knowledge of the alleged commission. Vera's informant declined to name his source. Sara, hospitalised with a fractured skull and other injuries, was unable to give any coherent account of events. Vera was very coherent and very angry about the loss of her fur coat. The vehicle in the case turned out to be a Daimler, reported missing the day before the incident by Theo Aristo, a well-known Sydney furrier.

In one of those strange lulls between royal commissions, with not even a murder or a media takeover to liven things up, the Missing Lynx Scandal took off like a rocket. Headlines came thick and fast: *Drag Queen Attacks King's Guest; Feminists Chase Transvestite For Fur Coat; Ecstasy In Punch – Socialites Run Amok.*

And on it went.

Not surprisingly, the public was a bit confused. The small print revealed that a woman had been seriously injured in some strange female gathering in Double Bay, that a lynx coat was missing, and that Vera Stone-Marten was angry. *Lynx Still Missing – Reward,* the newspapers told us. It was known that Claude Bell had been named by Vera and Deidre, but he couldn't be found. Passing reference was made to feminist hysteria. The Daimler turned up stripped and abandoned in Tempe.

The case took a new turn when a journalist received an anonymous phone call. The caller claimed to be in possession of the Missing Lynx, further asserting that the lining was packed with cocaine. He said the coat could be picked up in a locker at Wynyard station, and gave details. The locker proved to be empty. The newspapers were undeterred. *Feminist Drug Shock; Lynx – Drug Link,* gave us more food for thought. *Honi Soit,* Sydney University's student newspaper excelled itself with the headline: *Daimler Ex Machina Takes Double Bay Drug Haul.*

Sara, often described as a rampant feminist, had failed to elicit much sympathy with all the publicity. Having done a lot of investigative journalistic work involving police and politicians, she'd made quite a few enemies and had been sacked from several newspapers. She was nobody's favourite.

On the other hand, Bell had always been a popular and charismatic man, with friends in high places. He was often in the news for his doings. He was wealthy, a bit outrageous at times, but a philanthropist and benefactor of numerous charities and worthy causes. Personality profiles appeared in the press. We heard from his ex-wife in an article entitled, "My Love For Claude". Even his grandmother was resurrected from a nursing home to wax lyrical. "Claude is an angel," she told us. But this paragon of all virtues was yet to materialise.

Three days later, materialise he did, "surprised and shocked" by his reception. Having been on an outback property with friends, "getting away from it all", he'd missed the whole show.

Bell was interviewed by police, his fingerprints taken and identification parades organised. But, it seemed, nothing was produced to implicate him in the incident. And he had an alibi. The police kept up their efforts to find the culprit. *SPIV* proved to be a dead end, we were told and, it seemed, Vera's informant could be of no further help. So the whole thing dropped into the background as far as the media were concerned.

I'd forgotten about it, although Deirdre bashed my ear on the subject from time to time. Months went by and Bell was in the news again, lobbying for a green, anti-development group. Polly had gone on to bigger things and was standing as an independent in the upcoming State election. She was pushing a strong anti-corruption, anti-development line, and had put both sides of politics on notice that she would be tough. Some people thought she might end up with the balance of power.

One morning over breakfast I was surprised to see the headline: *Missing Lynx – Package Found*. I immediately felt pleased for Vera, thinking the coat had probably turned up under a seat in a railway carriage somewhere. But the article revealed a somewhat different box of tricks. It was dynamite.

This little number had apparently fallen off the back of a baker's cart in Macquarie Street, landing at the feet of the Opposition Leader. It contained a statutory declaration from a retired police officer (recently deceased) stating that evidence had been fudged in the Missing Lynx investigation. Other fingerprints had been substituted for Bell's at a critical stage of the inquiry, and various leads, like the *SPIV* angle, had been sabotaged. The package provided the original print evidence and also some interesting snaps of Bell and Polly King in what divorce lawyers used to describe as a compromising situation. It also revealed that the policeman in charge of the case was an old friend of Bell's.

On the strength of these developments and their investigation, Bell was eventually charged and committed for trial on the charge of assault occasioning grievous bodily harm. Other matters relating to bribery and the fudging of evidence were still being investigated.

I was asked to take the case.

10

The Verdict

As soon as it became known I would be defending Bell, I had Deirdre fuming across my desk.

"You're not going to defend that louse, are you?"

"Why not? Someone has to do it."

"How can you defend a gatecrashing, aggressive swine like him?"

"He wasn't a gatecrasher. Polly invited him."

"So what! He had no right to be there."

"I'll probably lose anyway. Calm down."

"And so you should. He's guilty."

"Only the good have no need of an advocate."

"Oh don't give me that classical crap, Mavis. Look, if you go through with this I'll never speak to you again."

"You shouldn't be talking to me now – you're a witness."

I looked her straight in the eye. "Have you ever been cross-examined by a top barrister?"

She glared at me, gathered her things, and made for the door. I watched her from the doorway as she stalked down the corridor.

"See you in court," I called after her.

At that moment Bob appeared in the corridor. Deirdre snapped at him: "That person ought to be locked up!" and stormed into the lift.

Bob looked at me. "A hostile witness, eh?"

"You bet," I replied.

We laughed and Bob returned to his rooms. The next thing I knew, Colette had turned up.

"Darling, I've been in touch with Cicero."

I froze.

"Not that layabout from Darling Point. I mean the real Cicero – at a challenging session."

"You're not getting him mixed up with Virgil again, are you?"

"No pet, I'm off the booze for good."

"Glad to hear it." I stretched. "So, what did Cicero have to say for himself?"

"He sends his compliments."

I straightened up. "Look you can cut the flummery, sweetie. I've got a lot on my mind –"

Colette cut in. "Hang on a minute. He spoke about Bell...he's as guilty as hell, but you'll win the case."

"Umm, that's an interesting opinion. Thanks, old girl. Why is Cicero so interested?"

"He takes quite an interest in us down here. He's seen it all before – reminds him of the bad old days in Rome. It's comic relief."

"I'm glad we are amusing somebody. God, there's no accounting for taste, is there? I'd go for the Marx Brothers any day. And how's Virgil?"

Colette seemed worried. "Oh, I haven't been able to reach him. He's showing Dante around the Underworld –"

I interrupted. "Sweetheart, I was referring to your friend, the marmalade charmer. How is he?"

Colette looked profoundly relieved. "Oh him. He's fine."

Two months later, the case began. The plea was self-defence. I intended to show the jury that, under the circumstances, Bell had used reasonable force to get out of the situation.

In the event, Bell was a defence lawyer's dream: articulate, persuasive, plausible. Polly had invited him to the gathering as a joke, and a friend from *SPIV* thought there might be an article in it. He had planned to reveal himself later in the evening, but he wasn't given the chance. It was just a harmless prank, but the ladies had become aggressive and threatened him. Beside the pool he had tried to escape but the situation got out of hand. He was surrounded, and Vera had produced a hatpin. He admitted pushing Sara in order to escape, but denied striking her.

The chief prosecution witnesses – Vera, Deirdre and Sara – I demolished. They denied all knowledge of a hatpin. But I managed to needle Deirdre till she blew her stack and started abusing me. This display on her part didn't impress the jury one little bit. In Vera's case I demonstrated that she was very angry at the time, and was far more interested in her fur coat than any injury to Sara. As to Sara, she had suffered memory lapses since the incident, and could give no clear account of events.

The judge summed up, telling the jury it was up to them to decide whether or not Bell had justified his self-defence plea.

The jury retired, deliberated, and returned. The verdict – not guilty.

11

Going Up

For me the Bell case was the turning point. I became a prominent criminal lawyer very much in demand. Every man and his dog thought I could get them off. This wasn't always true, but I established a formidable reputation. I took silk (became a Queen's Counsel) very early – one of the youngest in history.

I moved out of Alexandria, where I'd been living with Colette, and picked up a little place of my own at Point Piper. By this time, my old friends Matron and Ted had emigrated from Wilcannia and were looking for employment. So, after a series of disastrous housekeepers, I decided to give them a break. I took them both on as caretakers and general minders at Point Piper. Matron and I buried the hatchet. We got on famously.

Deirdre and I lost contact with each other. She had some sort of bust-up with Stray Liberation and seemed to be struggling. Lurching through a series of unworthy causes she ended up as president of the Save the Subjunctive Foundation, but this turned out to be an iffy proposition as well. Eventually she resorted to capitalism and started managing a stable of people on the lecture circuit. Dix Enterprises was very successful. Needless to say, I wasn't on the books.

In any case I was very busy being a big defence barrister. But, after a while, just to make life interesting, I changed sides and became a Crown Prosecutor. I found it suited my temperament better in many ways. Colette had kept in touch with Cicero and got lots of useful tips for me. I successfully prosecuted quite a few big names in the criminal world and, in the process, became good mates with the Attorney General and the Minister for Police.

"I'll clean up the state for you," I said. "You get them into court, and I'll nail them."

For a while New South Wales was in serious danger of going straight. But I'm exaggerating. There was still lots to do. And I hadn't nailed the one I really wanted. We all had our theories about Mr Big, and I was no exception. The boy I had in mind was very big indeed. I'd studied him from all angles trying to find a weakness, but there was never any real evidence.

He was into everything. Starting off as a bricklayer in a country town, he'd risen to fame in property development, transport, media, film production, horseracing, and that was just the legal stuff. Basically he lived by the three Ts – trusts, transport, and television.

He was suspected of having mafia and CIA connections and, over the years, had been friendly with several powerful politicians. In fact he'd been knighted along the way. Sir Hugh Bono graced many a table on the right side of town. But to his friends he was just Hughie.

Hughie Bono was the man to get, as far as I was concerned. He'd been pally with the Prime Minister, Rex Falcon, but had fallen out with him. No one was exactly sure why. It was rumoured the PM had given him the thumbs down on a casino for Parliament House. But that was just speculation.

Having dropped the PM, Bono forged various other powerful friendships. In particular, with Peter Banks, the Treasurer and heir apparent,

The Goddess Strikes Back

and with George Drover, the Minister for Foreign Affairs, who had never got over being ousted from the party leadership by the PM. I'd noted these friendships with interest.

Bono was a true bipartisan. He had friends in the opposition as well and was often on the guest list of Ian Brewer, the new leader. Ian had been drafted from the private sector to get the Opposition back on the rails after a long series of election defeats. The PM seemed to be invincible.

I'd become friendly with the PM, and warned him about Bono. Perhaps I'd had some effect. In any case, the PM and I became very good mates. We'd clicked as soon as we met. When in Canberra, I stayed at the Lodge, and when he was in Sydney I always popped into Kirribilli House. And, if the lights were on, I'd usually slip next door to Admiralty House to say hello to the Governor General. I was a bit of a bipartisan myself.

The PM and I would have long talks going far into the night. He was fascinated by my past lives. We'd talk of the pharaohs, Caesar, Wolsey, Lawrence, politics and power, life and death.

I'll always remember that particular night.

The PM spoke: "You know, Mave, I can empathise with Caesar. I've got enemies. Peter Banks wants my job, George Drover hates my guts, Bono would stab me in the back if he could. Brewer can't wait to have an election, the people are becoming restless and ungrateful."

"Don't be morbid, Prime Minister," I said. "You've got the top job. They can't touch you. Just ride it out."

Then to change the subject I said: "Seen any good movies lately?"

"As a matter of fact I'm off to Silverton the day after tomorrow to visit a movie set."

"Silverton's a long way away."

"I'm helping out a mate with some promotion. It's his first film. There'll be a few photo opportunities and a bit of fun."

"What's the film?"

"It's called *Madness at Milparinka*."

"That should keep them away in droves. What's it about?"

He shuffled through some papers. "I've got the prospectus for investors here somewhere…oh yes, here it is…it's an existentialist analysis of Sturt's expedition into the Stony Desert."

I broke up. "You mean an existentialist tax rort, don't you?"

"Oh don't be like that, Mavis. Mark Cass, the director, is a friend of mine. He's a good bloke. And I'm going to shake hands with Sturt."

"Resurrection in the desert, eh?"

"An actor who plays Sturt will shake hands with me – the Father of Australian Exploration meets the Father of Australian Consensus. Like it? Great photo opportunity. Do you want to come along?"

"I gatecrashed on Sturt once before. No, you desert fathers can have it all to yourselves this time."

And so the matter was dropped and we got onto other things. I can remember laughing and joking far into the night. Two days later neither of us was laughing. Events had taken an extraordinary turn.

12

The Ides of March

I awoke from a nightmare...the phone was ringing. It was very late. From my spot on the lounge I saw Matron stumbling across the room in the darkness. She turned on the lamp and picked up the phone.

"Hello, Mavis's residence...yes...oh, hello Joyce. Is anything wrong? Must be after midnight...yes...yes...heavens...yes...yes...hang on a tick, will you?" Matron looked worried. She moved the phone away from her mouth and said in a loud whisper: "It's Joyce from The Entrance...she thinks she's on to Mr Big!"

"Well I hope she has a great night," I replied. "Now do you mind if I get some sleep?"

The Goddess Strikes Back

"I don't mean that...she's got something on tape...there's a conspiracy...the Prime Minister's in danger...an ambush...something about a movie set in Silverton –"

"Oh for crying out loud!" I exploded. "The woman's raving. Tell her to have an aspirin and go back to bed!"

Ted emerged from the bedroom. "What's wrong?"

"Nothing," I replied.

Matron was speaking into the phone again: "She can't talk now, sweetie...no don't play it to me now...we'll call you in the morning...things will look different then...don't be silly, of course it won't be too late...stop worrying...have a whisky and get a good night's sleep...yes...will do...okay darling...bye-bye."

Matron turned to me. "She's really worried. She says she's got Hughie Bono on tape from his car phone...someone talking to him from Broken Hill –"

My ears pricked up. "Hughie Bono?"

"You always said he was Mr Big, didn't you?"

"Yes, and Joyce reckons she's got him on tape?"

"That's what she said. She knows his voice from other tapes she's got."

"Other tapes...of Bono?"

Matron was starting to look rattled. "Oh I don't know, Mavis. It's hard to get much sense out of Joyce sometimes."

"Exactly. She's off her rocker. Have you ever heard anything important on Joyce's tapes?"

"No, but she seemed so upset. She says they're planning to assassinate the PM on the movie set, with poisoned limes..."

"Poisoned limes! Oh, come on, I'm sure the PM'll be safe in Silverton." I yawned. "Now I've really got to get some sleep."

Matron turned off the lamp and they both went back to bed.

I lay there for a few minutes, expecting to drift off. But I was wide awake. I couldn't stop thinking about Joyce. She wasn't one of my favourite people. A sad case really, but dangerous. As a telephonist addicted to eavesdropping she'd terrorised Wilcannia and surrounding districts for years. Intercepting, relaying gossip, making and breaking reputations, she'd wreaked havoc. With the advance of technology she'd been able to make recordings as well.

Having retired early after a car accident, she'd gone into deep depression. Without a telephone exchange she was lost. Luckily her husband was an electronics buff. In desperation he gave her a scanner for their twenty-fifth wedding anniversary and saved her sanity. She could lock into any frequency – police, CB radio, Flying Doctor, School of the Air. She was the best informed woman west of the Darling. Not only could she scan, she recorded the results on a high-tech tape recorder. They'd moved to The Entrance, and Joyce did some casual work for Telstra. So I feared for the Central Coast. I'd warned her she could end up in jail for her antics, but she didn't take any notice. And now this. Could she, by some stroke of fate, actually have Bono on tape?

Pigs might fly!

A violent gust of wind lashed the balcony, blowing the door ajar. I hopped off the lounge and padded out to investigate. Everything seemed fine. I marvelled at the view – moonlight shimmering on the harbour, lights twinkling. What a spot! I'd come a long way from Heartbreak Corner and Wilcannia. I'd made it. But somehow Joyce had brought back all the old memories – heat, flies, gossip, and a nagging unease in the pit of my stomach. And what was that nightmare I'd woken from? I couldn't remember. The PM couldn't really be in danger, could he?

A flash of light filled the sky followed by a deafening crash. A bad storm was brewing. I hated storms. But everything went quiet again. I checked out the plants on the balcony and was surprised to find a dead wren behind one of the pots. Then came more lightning and thunder. The whole sky lit up. I was startled as a shape plummeted through the air and landed on the balcony beside me. A sparrow: as dead as a doornail. There was something in its beak. I looked closely – it was a sprig of laurel. I felt cold. An unnamed dread, as old as Egypt, fingered me. I shivered and looked back into the living room.

For some reason I noticed the calendar. The date leapt out at me – the fifteenth of March. The Ides of March! I knew immediately. I was inside in a flash.

"Matron," I shouted, "have you got Joyce's phone number?"

I flew to The Entrance by helicopter and heard the tape at 2.30 a.m. Bono or not, there was enough to ring the Attorney General.

13

Hughie Bono

A dawn raid on a movie set in Silverton averted a catastrophe. But not before a monumental stuff-up. It seemed *Madness at Milparinka* wasn't the only movie on the go at Silverton. And the director of *Burke and Wills Revisited* was none too pleased at having the fridge in his trailer raided by coppers looking for a basket full of limes. A couple of frantic phone calls revealed the mistake. Eventually the right director was found and the limes in his fridge were confiscated. One of these was later discovered to contain enough *Clostridium botulinum* to kill every prime minister from Barton onwards. But I'm getting ahead of myself.

In her routine scanning on the night of the fourteenth, Joyce had picked up a long-distance call from Broken Hill transmitted to Bono's car phone. The call related to a planned assassination of the Prime Minister. The caller, later identified as Mark Cass, the director, had lost his nerve. He wanted out of the conspiracy. Bono was angry. In the heat of the conversation discretion went out the window. Incriminating details emerged. Bono made it clear Cass's life was on the line if he pulled out. Cass reluctantly agreed to go ahead. Enter Joyce.

The limes were rushed to Broken Hill for analysis. In the meantime director, cast, and crew were all rounded up and held for questioning. When the results of the analysis came through, things hotted up. Type E *Clostridium botulinum* is a deadly poison causing botulism. Symptoms would not appear for twelve to thirty-six hours and diagnosis would be tricky. By that time any evidence at Silverton would have vanished.

The police leant very heavily on Cass. Eventually he cracked under pressure and admitted he was the speaker on the recording. In return for indemnity he spilled the beans and revealed Bono as the other speaker. Bono had promised Cass, a struggling new director, unlimited finance for his films in return for a "favour". So the PM would have sipped his spiked lime juice with Sturt in a publicity shot, and become history himself very quickly.

I had wanted to hold Bono immediately, but until the limes were analysed and Cass confessed, no one had taken the story seriously. By the time Cass confessed, Bono had taken a holiday. So did the tabloids: *Mafia Movie Scam – Plot To Kill PM; Big Shot Bugged – Phone Call from the Wrong Side; Invalid Telephonist Tapes Bono; Ides of March Conspiracy Flops; Signs and Portents Save PM.*

Cass was under heavy protection. So was Joyce. I was furious that we'd let Bono slip through our fingers. His disappearance was a terrible embarrassment. It seemed he'd left Australia on a false passport. Nobody knew where he was. Interpol had been alerted, but so far there were no leads.

Joyce was granted indemnity in return for eighteen suitcases of tapes and recording equipment – the work of a lifetime. All these were thoroughly investigated. Thanks to Joyce, the Rogers and Hart songbook enjoyed a renaissance at the Bureau of Criminal Intelligence. For hours at a time strains of "Mountain Greenery" and "My Funny Valentine" could be heard wafting through offices and corridors, which must have been a relief after days of fire brigade, CB radio, and School of the Air. "Bewitched, Bothered and Bewildered" was declared the all-time favourite. But Rogers and Hart weren't the only starters. Word got around that Frank Sinatra was in strife again – it being alleged that "Strangers in the Night" played backwards was a mafia manifesto. But that turned out to be a joke.

So, apart from renewing our acquaintance with the favourites of the forties, what did the tapes reveal? She'd picked up Bono and others here and there – a bit of race fixing and political wheeling and dealing. Enough for another couple of charges if needed. Apart from this? Nothing much. We learnt of a shady opal deal in White Cliffs in 1968, and rheumatologists would have a field day at Woy Woy. But overall we were bitterly disappointed.

"We've got to get Bono!" I told the Attorney General.

"The police are working day and night," he told me. "We've narrowed it down to the northern hemisphere."

I liked the Attorney General too much to reply.

Interpol had agreed to put Bono on its twelve most wanted list. News came through of sightings

The Goddess Strikes Back

in England, France, Scotland, Greece, Spain, Ireland, but never an arrest. There was even a theory that he'd never left Australia – that he was alive and well and living in Fingal. My friends from the Cave assured me this was nonsense.

Matron was monitoring things very closely.

One day she ran into my study exclaiming: "There's been a sighting near Loch Ness!"

I looked up. "What, Nessie lumbering through the bracken? Come on Matron, we're looking for Mr Big, not a prehistoric reptile...although come to think of it..."

"Bono was seen getting into a shiny cigar-shaped vehicle in a field near Loch Ness."

"Bono in a UFO. Quick, ring the *Telegraph*!"

"You're taking this very lightly, Mavis."

"It's the valium, Matron. Thanks."

The phone rang. Matron answered it, then spoke to me.

"It's Deirdre Dix...will you talk to her?"

"It's been a long time. She's got a nose for drama, I'll say that for her. Yes, I'll have a chat. Just as well I'm on medication."

Matron handed me the phone.

"Hello Deirdre, long time no see. What have you been up to? I mean apart from 'redefining in the gender contract', darling."

We had a pleasant enough chat and I invited her over.

The next day the three of us were sitting in the sun on the balcony.

"How's the search for Bono really going?" Deirdre asked.

"No good," I replied.

"How about doing the All stations to Thebes routine?" Matron suggested. "See what Hat has to say."

"I don't really want to keep going back to Hat with problems. I feel inept."

Deirdre said: "With half the ancient world under her thumb, she wouldn't be too impressed with this little lot. She'd eat Bono for breakfast."

Matron spoke: "I've got another idea."

"We're all ears," I replied.

"What about Cicero?"

"What about him?" I said.

"I mean Colette's Cicero. Isn't he keeping an eye on us down here? Maybe he knows where Bono is. Couldn't Colette go into a channelling session for us?"

I thought for a minute. "It's worth a try. Everything else has failed. I'll have to tell the PM and the police, and I'll have to talk Colette around."

The Goddess Strikes Back

The PM and the police were all for it. So Deirdre and I drove to Alexandria to talk to Colette.

Colette came out to meet and greet us. "When I saw the Jag, I knew it was you."

We walked inside. After a minute's pause I said: "Sit down, sweetie. I want to talk to you."

"I am sitting, Mavis."

"Oh, sorry love, I've got a lot on my mind."

I put forward the proposal. After some hesitation she agreed. But she was nervous.

"I've never had such a big responsibility," she said. "I'll have to be at home here in Alexandria. No hassles. No hurrying."

So it was set up. Colette and Matron in Alexandria; Deirdre and I at Point Piper. We had a special phone installed. All calls on my ordinary line were diverted to an answering service. It was all top secret and low key. There was to be one plain-clothed man outside Colette's place. They couldn't resist sending over some smoked salmon and chardonnay. Matron thanked them in a whisper and disappeared inside.

For some reason I thought we'd get the answer quickly. I'd invited the PM, the Attorney General and the head of the Australian Federal Police over for lunch, so we could all be together when the news came. They were running late. Ted was in the kitchen preparing lunch. Deirdre and I sat by the silent phone. She was very edgy.

"Sitting here staring at the bloody phone. It's like those movies where somebody's in death row," she said. "Remember Susan Hayward in *I Want to Live*? The gas chamber's only hours away…the governor hasn't called…everyone's waiting – warders, nurses, the priest…suddenly the phone rings –"

There was a knock at the door. We both jumped in fright. Ted ushered in our guests and offered drinks.

After introductions, the PM asked: "What's for lunch?"

"Oh, how can you think about food at a time like this!" Deirdre wailed.

The PM looked a bit surprised. "We've got to keep our strength up," he said lightly.

I reassured him. "Don't worry, PM – she's Susan Hayward waiting for a reprieve. Don't pay any attention to her."

Addressing Deirdre I said: "Go and help Ted in the kitchen. Make yourself useful."

She glared at me and flounced out of the room.

Everything was set up. Staff and bodyguards were hovering. Any urgent messages would come to the PM's car phone outside. We had a long lunch followed by billiards, then some mini golf in the backyard. Staff brought in a few messages from time to time. About three o'clock we all went out onto the balcony to enjoy the view – the harbour, trees, people.

The head of the Federal Police asked: "Where were you when you saw the signs and portents, Mavis?"

I showed him.

He continued: "Then you looked over your shoulder towards the living room?"

"Gee, I'd better get this right, hadn't I?" We all laughed.

The afternoon dragged on. The clock ticked. Dogs barked. Suddenly the phone shrieked. I ran to answer it.

"Hullo, yes, Matron...What? Oh a deep trance! Thank God for that, I thought you said a deep trench! Nothing doing yet, eh? That's okay, don't worry. Cicero's probably a very busy man – there's no statute of limitations where he is. The best idea might be not to ring till you've got an answer, that's easier for you and us. Right...bye."

We were all disappointed.

Deirdre exclaimed: "You cops and lawyers are all the same. You can never find one when you want one!"

We called it a day.

"I'll be in touch as soon as we get something," I told the PM.

Days went by. Nothing. To get my mind off things I accepted an invitation to the opera – Verdi's *The Force of Destiny*. I liked the sound of it. I let Matron know where I'd be, just in case.

At interval, feeling carefree for the first time in weeks, I laughed and joked over the bubbly, enjoying the moon-splashed harbour. Suddenly an usher touched my elbow. Thinking he wanted my autograph I said breezily: "Yes, sweetie?"

"Mavis, there's a phone call for you."

I sobered up and followed him to the office.

I picked up the phone. It was Matron. "Hullo Mavis, I'm ringing from a public phone, just to be safe. Our message has come through. Are you ready?"

"Of course."

There was a pause.

"I'll keep it short. 'Rome Opera, *Pagliacci*, next Tuesday night'. Got it?"

"Our birdie's going to the opera, is he?"

"So it seems."

"No mistakes?" I asked carefully.

"Rock solid, Mavis. A dead cert."

"Thanks, Matron. And if you get a chance, send my compliments to our informant."

"I will."

And so it went. At the first interval, after Pavarotti's stirring rendition of "On with the Motley", Bono was escorted to the cloakroom by the Rome police.

14

Playing Myself

I had intended to throw the book at Bono, or what was left of it after the extradition proceedings were completed, and if he hadn't died of food poisoning on the way back to Australia it would have been the case of my career.

I cracked up. They had me on intravenous valium for six weeks. When you let the biggest rat of your career slip from your clutches, you start to wonder what it's all about.

But Joyce was fine. She became a minor celebrity for a while. We ended up together again doing a national tour of TV chat shows, radio talkback and the like, telling the story of how we nearly caught Bono. We were on tour for about three weeks, staying at five-star hotels and living in style. I'd been told to keep an eye on her.

Twin accommodation with Joyce was a high-risk operation. I was frightened to use the phone, I can tell you. The sight of Joyce lying in bed, eyes closed, earphones in place, was a chilling experience. While on tour she told me she'd kept a few recordings up her sleeve for old times' sake. What do you do?

"It's mostly music," she said. "I need some entertainment. I've got them here." She pointed to her overnight bag. "Feel free to play them. They're all labelled. There's a player with them."

One night when I was alone in the hotel room I did look through her audio collection, as much out of boredom as anything else. There didn't seem to be much of interest. I settled down with a gin and tonic and started to listen to a Glen Miller medley. It seemed Joyce had some taste.

But somewhere between "Moonlight Serenade" and "Tuxedo Junction" a funny thing happened. Amid a lot of background noise and random sounds from the airwaves, a conversation was in progress.

"We've got to get the bastard out!" a familiar voice was saying. "Can we make the Bacchus story stick?"

"Not enough evidence at this stage," a second voice replied.

I recognised Bono as the first speaker.

Bono continued: "That's bad luck. A spy scandal would really finish him. One of the boys in the KGB, eh? Codenamed 'Bacchus' – the god of wine and theatre. Could be anybody! Are you sure you lot in the company couldn't bring it off?"

"Not at this stage. We're sure there's a mole, but we can't identify him."

"I can't wait any longer. It's got to be assassination – clean, decisive and soon. Operation Caesar must go ahead. They can't last once Falcon's gone. I want Brewer in charge. Banks thinks I want him – silly bastard."

"How much does Brewer know?"

"He knows about Bacchus. Nothing else."

"He's in for a pleasant surprise – the prime ministership on a platter. Okay, go ahead. We're behind you all the way. And one last thought…how about Drover for Governor General?"

Gales of laughter faded into static.

I poured myself a stiff gin and sat down again.

Bono had been clever, keeping both Brewer and Banks onside. Whoever became Prime Minister, Bono would be okay. But what about 'Bacchus'?

The Goddess Strikes Back

Bacchus, the god of joy and ecstasy. Was there really a spy, code-named Bacchus, whose exposure would rock the government? Bono and Brewer knew about him, and so did the CIA – the Company. Bono's friend on the phone was apparently one of them. Bono wanted Falcon out for his own reasons and the CIA would support him for theirs. But the assassination plot had failed. 'Bacchus' sounded like a very dangerous time bomb. When would it detonate?

Then I thought of Joyce. Did she know what she had? I'd have to test her out.

Later that night when she came in, we chatted for a while.

"By the way, I played your Glen Miller tape."

"Oh, I'd forgotten about that one," she said.

"May I borrow it when we get back home?"

Not a flicker of interest. "Keep it. I never play it now."

Joyce had bombed badly. I decided to bide my time and play it cool.

We survived the tour somehow. Joyce returned to The Entrance and I went back to the bar. I took my share of briefs, but my heart wasn't in it. There was talk of a mini-series, but I put my foot down. You've got to draw the line somewhere, haven't you?

A big plus at that period was my deepening friendship with Rex Falcon. He was very grateful to me for saving his life and offered me jobs of all descriptions. But I didn't want to take the jump too quickly, so I stalled a bit. As a special token of his esteem he commissioned a sculpture for the Sturt National Park: the *Mother of Australian Exploration*. I had many long sittings for that one.

I used to pop in to the Lodge quite often and we'd talk.

"You've changed the course of history, Mavis," he said. "Our destinies are intertwined."

"Yes, Prime Minister," I replied.

He looked at me sharply. "Never use that phrase, Mavis. It makes me nervous."

Then just at the right time I was offered a movie role. After the debacle of *Madness at Milparinka* the industry still wanted to have a go at the outback. So I was asked to play myself in an historical extravaganza called *Menindee Magic*, a more light-hearted treatment of the journey into the interior.

The Australian premiere coincided with the unveiling of the *Mother of Australian Exploration* at Fort Grey. Everything worked brilliantly. The movie made quite a splash on the international market. We went on a big promotional tour of the

US, which was great fun. I visited Rex and Octavia in LA. Everything was terrific. As a matter of fact I got an Oscar nomination for best actress, but was pipped at the post by someone, I forget her name, in a remake of *Cleopatra*. Well, you can't win them all.

15

The Political Stage

As soon as I got back from the States, the PM was on the phone.

"Hi, Mave. How are you? I want you to join the party and head the New South Wales Senate ticket at the next election. With your drawing power we could easily pick up a third seat."

"The Senate? I'm all for life after death, but I plan to enjoy it!"

"Oh, be a sport. We're struggling in the polls. We need a drawcard. You'd be perfect. You're the most popular person in Australia – next to me, that is."

"Not interested."

The Goddess Strikes Back

"What about the Reps? Pick your seat – it's yours. We'll put you into the ministry as soon as you're elected."

"I'm a loner, not a joiner, Prime Minister. Sorry. And caucus doesn't like tall poppies anyway."

He tried to talk me around, but I was adamant.

Later on I was telling Deirdre about it. Her eyes were gleaming. She paced the room, chain smoking.

"You're crazy," she said. "You should have accepted. I'd be your campaign manager, like the old days in Stray Liberation."

"I'm not interested, Deirdre," I said, yawning.

She stopped pacing. "Why not be an Independent? You could stand for the Senate as an Independent. It'll be a close election. You might end up with the balance of power."

A light gleamed at the back of my mind.

"The balance of power," I murmured, "that could be interesting."

"It'd be terrific," Deirdre said. "You'd have everyone at your mercy."

"But I'd have to share the balance with somebody, the way the numbers go."

"We could work it out," she said. "Hope for somebody malleable."

The subject was dropped for a while, then a funny thing happened. The PM announced the appointment of his vanquished opponent George Drover, as Governor General. After I'd stopped laughing, I realised that this development, along with the Opposition having control of the Senate, could make life very interesting.

Not long after Drover took up residence at Yarralumla, the PM asked him for a double dissolution. No problems. We were suddenly in election mode. I knew my time had come.

To a packed press conference I announced I would be standing for the Senate as an Independent for the State of New South Wales.

"What's your platform?" they asked. "What are you for, and what are you against?"

"I'm for cleaning up Australia. I'm for balance and reason, I'm for stopping the rot."

"Will you be a fence sitter?"

I threw the questioner a withering glance.

"Will you be a good watchdog?"

"What if you get the balance of power?"

The questions came thick and fast.

After twenty minutes Deirdre stepped in. "Mavis is tired," she said.

My campaign moved into top gear pretty quickly. Deirdre was my campaign manager and ideas person. Colette, Matron, and Ted volunteered their services full-time, along with hundreds of other fans throughout the state. Donations came flooding in from all over the place. And, of course, I provided a bit of finance myself.

We opened the campaign with a big party at Fort Grey, with the *Mother of Australian Exploration* looking on. Then we had a camel race to Tibooburra, and from there a chartered jet took us to Wilcannia, for a reception at the museum redecorated in 1880s style with everyone in period costume playing historical identities. The New South Wales sales manager of Carton and United, playing Edmund Resch, accompanied me and the local mayor, playing EBL Dickens, on a parade through town ending in a giant beer-fest on the river. The next day we went by barge down to Menindee. Crowds lined the Darling as never before in history. In the outback I was a smash hit.

For two weeks we toured the North Coast. It was a walkover.

"We've got to nail Sydney," Deirdre said. "The rest of the state's sewn up."

We got together with an advertising agency to discuss tactics. In the middle of the discussion Deirdre exclaimed: "We'll use your past lives!"

And so we devised a series of ads for prime time television.

The overall theme was: *Mavis: she's tough, she's honest – a proven record back to the Pharaohs.* We had toyed with the idea of getting the original footage from Hat, but we opted for a remake.

The ads went like this:

Friend to the Pharaohs
Martyred in Alexandria
Slaved in Medieval Slums with the Poor Man's Lawyer
Ruled Hampton Court for Cardinal Wolsey
Saved Sturt from Disaster in the Desert
Beloved of Queen Victoria
Fought Alongside Lawrence of Arabia
Foiled an Ides of March Assassination Conspiracy
Nearly Caught Mr Big

"What more could they want?" Deirdre said.

"You can axe the last one for a start," I replied.

Colette sprung into action and did a number of sittings with Cicero, collecting enough material for a series of articles in the quality press. The series, entitled *Why I'm Backing Mavis*, lifted circulation to equal the tabloids.

This encouraged other psychics into the fray, and before we knew where we were half of Ancient Rome were giving Australians political advice via the newspapers. Subeditors had a ball! *Psychic Civil War; Pompey Backs the*

Liberals; Caesar Stands Firm with Labor; Mark Antony Undecided.

One channeller maintained that Cicero would materialise in the national tally room on election night. Colette was furious.

"He wouldn't be seen dead in a place like that," she said.

Then, just when we thought the Roman connection had reached saturation point, there came a bombshell. Brian Tooth of *The Claw*, a radical, investigative monthly, published a leaked document from 'intelligence sources' alleging the existence of Bacchus. 'Bacchus' being the codename for a highly placed spy in the Department of Foreign Affairs. Tooth asserted the existence of Bacchus had been a well-kept secret in intelligence circles both here and overseas for some time. And not only intelligence circles, I thought.

Everyone went mad. Brewer was all innocence and righteous indignation. Tooth was taken to court, but wouldn't reveal his sources. There were official denials from the government, channellers pulled out all the stops for an all-out Bacchus hunt, and the opposition looked like romping home. I thought the government was finished.

And nobody was surprised at the headline right on the eve of the election: *Caligula's Horse*

Predicts a Landslide. People frantically bought out the edition only to find out the old boy was referring to an unexpected rock fall near the Bulli Pass. So, it's not over yet, I thought.

My own campaign had gone very well. I was confident. Election night was a knockout. By 10 p.m. I knew I had a quota. It was a history-making Senate vote. In the final count I got the primary vote of eighty-five per cent of voters. I hadn't directed preferences, so I had followers of all persuasions. I held a press conference at about 10.30, then went to the tally room to make my services available to broadcasters.

Colette was a guest commentator on one channel. There was a bit of comic relief when she had a stand-up fight with the expert psephologist Malcolm McDuck, about some surprisingly tight booths in Alexandria. Australia-wide, the result was "too close to call".

Much to Colette's relief, Cicero didn't show.

In the final shakedown the government scraped back in the Reps, with the Senate evenly divided: Government 37 – Opposition 37. The balance of power was held by my good self, and Dandy Duckworth, an animal liberationist from Tasmania.

Deirdre was very excited. "This'll be a walkover," she breathed.

16

The Rigours of Office

As I arrived at my Parliament House office Deirdre was putting a sign on the door. "No deals", it read.

"Good girl," I said.

On my desk was a set of dossiers Deirdre had compiled on people I'd be dealing with and needed to know about. The files were classified *Friends, Enemies, Pushovers, Unknowns, Idiots*. And there was a separate file labelled *Dandy Duckworth*.

"The only absolute certainty is Dandy," Deirdre said. "You've got her completely mesmerised."

"Yes, she's coming along nicely. If I told her to cool off in Lake Burley Griffin, she would."

Life in the old Rabbit Warren was hard to get used to. Deirdre consoled me with the thought that we'd soon be moving into the new parliament house.

"I hate moving house," I replied.

We had an office the size of a shoebox. Outside, the birds nearly drove me mad – pigeons, starlings, sparrows. Dandy was delighted, no doubt. On my first day I was dive-bombed by a magpie. Luckily nobody caught it on camera. Birds, no space, politicians, press. I must have been mad to get into this, I thought.

But the Senate Chamber itself was a dream. In its crimson comfort I felt very much at home. It was beaut for an afternoon nap, too. On my first day I stole the show by arriving in a silk gown and full bottomed wig – this gear being the prerogative of presidents of old. But strange garb is not unique to past presidents. When I first saw the Usher of the Black Rod (a sort of high class bouncer who looks after the Senate and its precincts), I nearly mistook him for Leopold Mozart. After getting over some initial confusion, we established a good working relationship. My time spent in the chamber was happy.

In the office it was a different story. For a start, phones were a problem. Some people told me to ignore the clicking sounds. Others informed me that ASIO taped all Parliament House calls. So just to keep them happy I had a regular dose of "From Russia with Love" piped through the system.

I was allowed a staff of four. In Canberra, Deirdre was my secretary, office manager and researcher. Ted was a minder, press secretary, and man Friday. In my Sydney office Colette and Matron did the lion's share. I decided to rotate my Sydney and Canberra staff because about every six weeks Deirdre and I went into meltdown mode and had to get away from each other.

Despite the sign on the door we were inundated with pressure groups. There were cases of Veuve Clicquot, crates of smoked salmon, and general grovelling – all to get me onside. I told everyone, including the press, that I would be voting on the issues, nothing else. The fact that I was a friend of the Prime Minister's was irrelevant.

I spent quite a bit of time in the PM's office, much to the chagrin of Brewer and the Opposition. I told the PM that Dandy and I would probably support him most of the time. I promised to keep Dandy in line but we both agreed we'd have to give her some leeway to keep her satisfied.

The PM seemed to be happy. He'd won the election, he was still leader, the 'Bacchus' story seemed to have died.

"Do you think there was anything in it?" I asked.

"No, a beat-up," he replied confidently.

Remembering Joyce's recording, I wondered. So I made a point of making the acquaintance of Charles Tape, the Director General of ASIO. Charles was a low-key type who didn't give much away. On the subject of Bacchus he was noncommittal.

I made a big effort with Ian Brewer. Given the numbers in the Senate he was naturally keen to get onside. I tolerated his attentions as best I could. One night over dinner, after he'd explained the joys of economic rationalism, I steered him on to intelligence matters. He boasted about his contacts in the CIA and British Intelligence.

"We've still got to be vigilant, despite *glasnost* and *perestroika*," he said.

"What do you make of the Bacchus story? Do your friends overseas know anything?"

He looked at me quickly. "No, I think it's a dead-end issue," he replied.

"Pity for you," I said. "With a real spy scandal you could reject Supply and romp home. With no money they would have to go to the people."

The Goddess Strikes Back

"I'd need your support," he said.

"Indeed you would," I replied.

I courted Peter Banks, treasurer, art lover, and aspirant to the top job. The PM seemed safe enough, but you could never be sure. If Peter ousted the PM I'd have to deal with him. I had Peter over for dinner a few times. We'd play CDs and talk about art and politics. We exchanged one or two Sotheby's catalogues. One night I nearly played him the Glen Miller medley, but thought better of it. I sounded him out about what he'd do if he became Prime Minister, policy wise.

"Economics is the big thing, Mavis. The market is what it's all about ultimately."

"Just lie back and think of Wall Street," I exclaimed.

I socialised quite a bit to keep in touch – Members' Bar, Non-Members' Bar, Dining Room, Library. I got to know a lot of people very quickly. I regularly did the rounds of cabinet ministers and their staffs. I admit I courted the Minister for Foreign Affairs. Colette had bent my ear about getting her a diplomatic job in Rome.

"I'll never ask you for another thing, darling," she said.

"I can't promise anything," I replied.

I was told we'd have to wait for a while for a suitable vacancy to come up.

Social life in Canberra can be great, if you know the right people. A real buzz was my regular visits to Yarralumla to see George Drover, the Governor General. I'd always thought things might be a bit tricky with George, me being such a good mate of the PM's, but he found me irresistible. I would go to Yarralumla whenever I needed a break, stay overnight, then drag George out of bed to see the sunrise.

My greatest find was Bill Clayton, the principal private secretary to the Minister for Foreign Affairs. I got to know him when I was courting the minister about a job for Colette. We clicked straight away.

Bill had an interesting history. From a working class background, he'd risen to become a Rhodes Scholar and academic. Later on he became a diplomat, doing stints in various parts of the world, including Rome and Cairo. Eventually he resigned from the diplomatic service and became an art collector and businessman. A man for all seasons, he had friends in business, the arts, the union movement, academia, and both sides of politics. Then he surprised everybody by joining the ALP and gaining preselection for a marginal seat. He entered parliament, but unfortunately lost his seat after one term. He then joined the staff of the Minister for Foreign Affairs.

During his days in Cairo, Bill developed a passion for all things Egyptian, and over the years had acquired an interesting collection of Egyptian antiquities. He had even been on a couple of archaeological digs.

"I'm a bit of an Egyptian antiquity myself," I told him.

"How much?" he asked.

"The lady's not for sale," I replied.

He sold me one of his favourite pieces, a bronze Egyptian cat. It cost me a packet, but it was worth it.

Colette insisted on meeting him, and we spent many an evening over the chardonnay talking about his days in Rome and Cairo, and looking at his collection. He promised Colette he'd fix up a Roman job for her.

We also enjoyed witty vignettes about people and places, particularly on matters political. I tried to get Deirdre interested.

"Why don't you come over one night?"

"No way," was the reply.

Life went on fairly comfortably for a while. Then came The Move. When I saw the office they'd given me in New Parliament House, I threatened to resign. I negotiated with friends in high places and got a better one, with a view. I don't really want to comment on the story about me and the Bogong moths. Let's just say it was greatly exaggerated.

Time slipped by. On the world stage we saw the crumbling of communism and the end of the Cold War. Bacchus might be out of a job, I thought. On the domestic scene the PM had problems. The government wasn't popular. There were rumblings about a second assassination plan. The newspapers were full of it, day in, day out.

Colette's appointment was announced. *Jobs for the Girls: Mavis's Mum Gets Plum Job in Rome*. It got the leadership issue off the front page, but there was a lot of criticism. Dandy was delighted at the appointment. Brewer hated it, but was frightened of getting me offside. Colette wasn't due to take up her appointment for another six months.

"I can't do anything right," the PM complained. He was getting demoralised. He doubled his security guard, employed more minders, including a taster to test all his food and drink.

"Nothing tastes any good when you think you're being poisoned," he told me.

"Yes, I remember Claudius saying that," I replied.

"A car backfires and I go to pieces."

"Yes, I know," I said. I seemed to have run out of encouragement.

Finally, the PM became ill.

"I'm being poisoned. I'm sure of it," he said.

"Brewer's getting a free ride. Your own people are doing you in!"

In an attempt to rally him I got some of my mates in the film industry to talk to him.

"You can star in your own life story," they told him.

"I already have," he replied.

Then I got some TV moguls in on the act.

"You can have your own show," they said.

"I've always had my own show."

"For God's sake make him an offer he can't refuse!" I shouted.

But nobody had one.

Then I happened to bump into Brian Tooth. Over a drink, we had a very interesting conversation.

I couldn't wait to get the PM on the phone.

"Prime Minister, I'd like you to come to dinner. There's something I want you to hear."

And so he got to hear the Glen Miller tape.

He was surprisingly calm. "Bono was more devious than I realised," he said.

"But what about Bacchus?"

"Bacchus is a dead issue, Mavis."

"Brian Tooth tells me it's a live issue that will explode soon." I continued: "Get out now, while you can. If there's a spy within cooee of the government, and he's exposed, you're all dead. Let Banks wear it – the spy scandal we had to have. See how he likes the hot seat. He wants the top job. Let him have it. If they don't get him on the economy, they'll dredge up Bacchus, for sure."

"The Cold War's over, Mavis. People aren't interested in spies anymore."

"I bet the CIA and ASIO wouldn't agree with you. Cold War or not, a spy smuggled into the government for the last few years would be a bit embarrassing, wouldn't it? He might even be in the cabinet. KGB files are turning up all over the place. You never know what might happen. Tooth says there'll be a defection soon."

"A defection?"

"Yes. And it'll make the Petrov case look like a Sunday school picnic."

He studied me as I continued: "Retire like a statesman. You can have your own chat show. I'll be your first guest. Discretion assured."

"I can't live on discretion, Mavis."

The Goddess Strikes Back

"I'll negotiate a deal for you. I'll get you an offer you can't refuse."

Soon afterwards the PM surprised everybody by giving up his political career and entering show business.

And thus the succession proceeded.

17

Bacchus

"Good morning, Prime Minister."

"Good morning, Senator."

Peter Banks was looking very well.

"So, the top job at last," I said.

"There's a lot to do."

"And you're just the boy to do it. Let me know if you need me."

"I will."

"Is Colette's job still on?"

"We might put it on the backburner, till we settle in a bit."

"Okay, I'll tell her."

So Banks took the reins.

The Goddess Strikes Back

Rex Falcon receded into the background for a while, then re-emerged with a very big show, an interview program entitled *Forty-Three Minutes*. He travelled the globe getting international names to be interviewed. A few home-grown celebrities got a guernsey. As a matter of fact, I was his first guest. I nearly broke the bank with the fee I charged.

"For you, anything," he said.

Peter Banks went from strength to strength. Brewer was beginning to look like an amateur.

"Brewer's got a fight on his hands," Deirdre said. "If he wants to win he'll have to pull something out of the hat."

"How about an Ancient Roman god?" I said.

"You've got Romans on the brain."

I ignored this and continued: "We've got supply bills coming up. I've always thought Brewer might turn on something at supply time."

"We'll soon see," Deirdre replied.

One morning I breezed into the Foreign Minister's office.

"Where's Bill?" I asked. "I've got great news. The Langton Collection is coming to Australia!"

The Minister looked tired and drawn.

"Bill's away for a few days, Mavis," he said.

"He didn't tell me he was going away. Where has he gone?"

"Just away…a family matter. Now what's this collection you're talking about?"

The Langton Collection, from the Petrie Museum in London. It's the biggest collection of Egyptian cats in the world."

"You mean dead ones," said one of the staff.

"I mean gold, silver, bronze, jewels – works of art, you idiot!"

I surveyed the outer office.

"You all look like death warmed up, yourselves," I said. "I think I'll leave you bunch of mummies to get on with your work."

With that I left. Outside in the corridor I stopped. It was that unmistakable feeling. Something was wrong. I walked back to my own office and called Deirdre in.

"There's something wrong in Foreign Affairs," I said.

"How do you mean?"

"Bill isn't there. They say he's away on a family matter. There's something about the office, you know, as if someone has carked it. I think we'll go over to Bill's place. Can you overcome your distaste and drive me, please?"

Bill had a lovely home in Sydney, but he kept a place in Canberra too. As we drove along the tree-lined street I noticed a vehicle parked near

Bill's place. As we drew closer I saw it was a Telstra van parked next door. Two men were in the neighbour's front garden.

"Keep driving, Deirdre. There's something wrong here."

"How do you mean?"

"Just keep driving. We'll go back to the office and come back later... That Telstra van's odd. Bill's neighbour is an academic. He's been overseas on sabbatical for months and he won't be back till next year. And I know he's not renting the place. So why would Telstra be there?"

"They always come at a bad time."

"But this is ridiculous, even for Telstra. I smell a rat, Deirdre. We'll go back later and see what's happening."

At dusk we returned. Obeying an instinct of mine, we left the car a couple of blocks away. The van had gone. Everything seemed to be clear. We had a key Bill had given me in case I needed it. We let ourselves in.

In the gloom the place felt eerie. We moved into the living room. Bill had some of his collection in his Canberra house. A statue of Anubis (the jackal-headed god of the Underworld) seemed to dominate the room.

"Where's the light? This place gives me the creeps," Deirdre said.

I pointed to the switch.

"Oh, that's better," she said, as light flooded the room.

I moved around quickly, examining his bookcases and furniture. A book entitled *The Eleusinian Mysteries* lay open on the coffee table. I moved around the rest of the house, taking Deirdre with me.

"Everything seems to be okay," I said. "I was half expecting a burglary."

I thought for a minute.

"Wait here, Deirdre. I'll be back in a moment."

I went next door and got inside via an opening in a back window. Someone had been through the place like a dose of salts. I returned to Deirdre.

"They've ransacked next door," I said. "Been through everything, broken into a safe, taken up floorboards, the lot. Put it all back, but they left traces…God, I need a drink."

I looked towards the liquor cabinet. Seated on it was a statue of my old friend Bastet, basket in hand, staring back at us.

"He wouldn't part with that one," I said.

We opened the cabinet. As always, it was chock-a-block.

"What'll it be?" Deirdre asked.

"I need a brandy," I replied.

"Why don't I make a fancy cocktail?" Deirdre rummaged through the cabinet, checking out the bottles. "Hang on, what's this?" she said. "It's an old recipe book."

Deirdre leafed through it. As she did, something fell out onto the floor. She picked it up.

"It's a postcard," she said.

"Okay, okay," I said. "Let's get on with the drinks. Give me the reading matter."

"So, *Vok Entertains*," I said, leafing through a slim glossy booklet produced by Jan Vok Liqueurs. "On second thoughts, I'll have a Black Lace."

After some discussion, Deirdre settled for a Sputnik.

We sat down. "Cheers."

I glanced idly at the postcard. It showed an unimaginative photo of the Sydney Harbour Bridge. Someone initialled "C" had written the following: *"Dear Bill, greetings from Sydney. I changed plans and went to the Tusculum Gallery's latest exhibition. Had an interesting discussion with the curator. Hope life is being good to you."*

We were on our second drink when Deirdre said she needed to go to the bathroom.

"Use the ensuite," I said. "It's got a better toilet."

While she was gone I sat and tried to outstare Anubis.

After a minute or two she returned to the living room looking puzzled. She handed me a crumpled sheet of paper.

"I found this in a corner of the ensuite."

It was a plain sheet of A4 paper containing a long series of numbers in groups, written in ballpoint pen. The numbers covered the whole sheet. The first six groups read: 1-2-7-12 1-2-4-6 1-2-8-5 1-2-5-3 1-2-3-2 1-2-7-7. There were one hundred and sixteen groups.

"It might be a coded message," I said.

"You mean the sort of thing spies go in for?"

I hesitated. "Not only spies."

"Bill's not a spy, is he?"

I groaned. "I hope not. But if he is, why would he leave a coded message around like this? He's bright...he must have wanted it found...or else he didn't care...or maybe it's rubbish."

I thought for a few minutes. "Deirdre, I think Telstra's burgled the wrong house."

"Oh?"

"For ages there's been a rumour about a spy in Foreign Affairs: Bill's disappeared, Foreign Affairs are in shock, there's a coded message in Bill's house, and ASIO has burgled next door."

The Goddess Strikes Back

"ASIO?"

"In disguise, of course. I bet they'll be back when they get the right number. Bill's seventeen, next door's nineteen – someone misread a seven for a nine; an easy enough mistake."

"I can see why you were a good defence barrister, but are you sure you're not jumping to conclusions about this?"

"It's a gut feeling. Dick, Bill's neighbour, is a stickler for privacy – keeps all his papers in a safe when he's away. They probably didn't realise their mistake till they got into the safe."

I handed Deirdre the sheet of paper.

"Go and put it back where you found it, and turn off the lights. We don't want anyone knowing we're here."

"What if it's incriminating evidence? Do you want Bill to be found out?"

"I don't know. Just put it back."

Deirdre obeyed.

We switched off the lights and sipped our drinks in twilight. I kept watch at the window.

A few minutes later a vehicle approached and slowed down. A van.

"Telstra's back," I whispered. "Let's go, we'll take our drinks and reading matter with us."

We left quietly by the back door. We went through several backyards to get to the car.

Back at the office we took stock.

"I'm going to talk to the PM," I said. "Get him on the phone, will you?"

Deirdre returned. "He's in conference for the rest of the night and can't be disturbed."

"Try the Foreign Minister."

Same answer. Likewise the Attorney General.

"See if you can get Charles Tape."

Word came back. "He's in conference too."

I rang Brian Tooth.

"What's going on, Brian?" I asked.

"You'll find out in a few days, Mavis," he said. "Watch out for a special edition of *The Claw*."

Beyond that, he wouldn't talk.

Next day I went to see the PM. He was reticent. He didn't want to discuss the matter.

"It's about Bill, isn't it?" He couldn't hide his response.

"Prime Minister, I know his place has been searched. He's disappeared. What's going on?"

"We've got to keep the lid on it for the time being," he said.

"Brian Tooth knows something."

"Stuff Brian Tooth!"

"I might be able to help."

"It's too big, Mavis. Even for you."

A couple of days later Brian Tooth broke the silence. *The Claw*, in a special edition, told us the story.

Vladimir Rakov, third secretary at the Russian Embassy, had defected. He was in fact a KGB colonel and had been their Chief Resident in Australia. The defection had taken place some weeks previously, and Rakov was still being debriefed by ASIO at a safe house in Canberra.

Rakov's original brief from Moscow had been to penetrate key organisations – political parties, government departments, unions, media – with a view to recruiting agents of influence in all areas. As part of his brief he had spent time in the Australia-USSR Friendship Society. In that organisation he had become friends with Dr Boris Beckett, a rheumatologist, who was treating him for a repetitive strain injury. Beckett was an office-holder in the Australian Medical Association, one of the many organisations he had been instructed to penetrate. Unbeknown to Rakov, Beckett was in fact a part-time ASIO operative who, it seemed, had succeeded in turning his opponent.

Rakov's chief bombshell had been revealing the identity of the spy, codenamed Bacchus, whose existence had so long been suspected. *The Claw* didn't name the spy, but it informed us he was on the staff of the Minister for Foreign Affairs, and had been a long-standing member of the ALP.

Given the gravity of Rakov's claims, the Director General of ASIO, Charles Tape, had briefed the Prime Minister and the National Intelligence and Security Committee (consisting of senior cabinet ministers and public servants) on the situation. The spy was to be put under surveillance, and before action was taken, it was seen as proper for the government to be informed. But, it seems, something had gone wrong. Bacchus was "missing".

Once Tooth published the story, all hell broke loose. Brewer and the Opposition went crazy. So did the media. I feared Brian might have gone too far, but he was unrepentant. Things moved very quickly. Within forty-eight hours we had a progression of headlines. From the mundane, *Defector Blows Bacchus*, to the witty, *Jobs for the Boys – In the KGB*, to the imaginative, *Yes, Virginia, Bacchus Does Exist*, ending with a highly personal, not to say ambiguous, *Mavis Mates with Mole*.

It had gone far enough for me.

18

The Ring of Three

I crashed straight into a meeting between the PM and Tape.

"What's going on?" I stormed.

"I'm going to make a statement this afternoon," the PM said.

"Not before time. Your committee's leaking like a sieve."

"That's a matter for judgement," the PM replied, casting a glance at Tape.

"Something's leaking. I've been implicated, and Bill Clayton's missing. It is Bill, isn't it? Is Bill Bacchus?"

"The evidence suggests that he is," Tape replied.

"I want the full story. There must be something Tooth doesn't know."

"There's a lot Tooth doesn't know," Tape said. He looked towards the PM.

"Go ahead," the PM said.

Tape continued: "Years ago Rakov spent time in the Illegal Section of the KGB's Foreign Intelligence Directorate in Moscow. It seems Clayton was recruited at that period while a university student. He has always been run by the Illegal Section and controlled by illegals."

"Illegals?"

"That means agents without diplomatic cover; agents not connected with the embassy. Those men would have some other cover in Australian life – academics, businessmen. His current controller is an illegal officer codenamed 'Lark'. Rakov doesn't know him or his cover identity."

Tape lit a cigarette and continued: "Rakov came to us with an enormous amount of documentation, including files smuggled by old friends from the tottering KGB. We've been working day and night, going through this material. There's still a mountain of it."

"Is there material to back up his story about Bill?"

"Yes, there are files that confirm Rakov's story."

"I can't believe it. So where's Bill? If you had proof, why didn't you bring him in straight away?"

"We had to be cautious. We weren't sure the files were authentic. It was political dynamite. We were hoping for corroboration. That's why we put him under surveillance."

"So how come he's missing?"

"Well may you ask," said the PM, looking at Tape coldly.

Tape was clearly embarrassed. "He was under surveillance, but I'm afraid he gave us the slip."

Silence.

"Tell her!" the Prime Minister thundered.

Tape cleared his throat. "Clayton went to a party."

"Yes?"

"A Halloween party in Sydney."

"Okay. So he went to a Halloween party in Sydney."

"In some fancy get-up – a toga, like an Ancient Roman."

"So?"

"Our chaps did their best. But sometime during the night he switched clothes with one of the other guests."

"Yes?"

"When they saw an Ancient Egyptian queen leaving the party, they naturally didn't make the connection."

It was painful listening. Around 4 a.m. discreet enquiries made to an inebriated lady in a toga revealed that Cicero and Queen Hatshepsut had decided to retire for a while, and re-emerged in exchanged costumes. The lady was unable to speculate on the whereabouts of her earlier partner, or the costume. All efforts to locate Clayton since then had failed.

I called for a double scotch.

"You'll never live this down, either of you," I said. "So we've got a defector, a missing spy, and a question mark over everyone who knew about Rakov's story. That's you two, the ministers and public servants on the Security Committee, senior ASIO people. And how come Brian Tooth knew so much?"

"What about yourself?" Tape said. "You seem to know a bit more than you should."

I countered by changing the subject. "What are you going to do now?"

"Try to control the damage and find out what's happened."

He reached for the inside pocket of his coat and produced a well-worn sheet of paper.

"We have one clue," he said, surveying the PM and me meaningfully.

Tape passed me the sheet. It looked like the one Deidre had found in Bill's ensuite. I pretended to be suitably surprised and interested. "What is it?"

"It was found in Clayton's house. It may be a coded message."

"It was rather careless of him to leave it behind," I observed.

Tape replied: "Of course it might be disinformation. On the other hand, it could be an important lead if we break the code."

"What about Rakov?"

"We're leaning on him. We're sifting his material very carefully. The embassy's line is that he had been recalled to Moscow for incompetence. He defected to save his reputation. They deny outright that he's KGB."

"So what does Bill's disappearance mean? Would Moscow want him?" I said.

"Now that the Cold War's over, he'd be an even bigger embarrassment to Moscow than he is to us."

"So he's gone into hiding of his own accord?"

"Maybe. We just don't know."

"But he knew he was blown."

"We don't see his disappearance as coincidental."

I was depressed and decided to change tack.

"What about the other documentation?"

"There's some very interesting stuff. Some going back to previous residents – profiles of various people in Australia, people Moscow wanted to cultivate. Some of them we already have files on ourselves. Rakov is examining all relevant files of ours. He says he can spot a spy immediately from his profile."

"So, let's get a side-on shot of everyone in Australia, and we're in business," I said.

Tape laughed. "I mean patterns in the life history, trends in the lifestyle –"

"Okay, Charles. I believe you."

I paused before continuing.

"What about the CIA and the British? Are they interested?"

"They're behind us all the way."

"Then you'd better watch your back."

I turned to the PM. "You're really in trouble. You've got supply bills coming up, haven't you?"

"Don't remind me, Mavis."

"Good luck with your statement."

"Thanks. I'll need it."

And sure enough, the next day, after the PM's revelations had sunk into the national psyche, Brewer came to see me in a righteous fervour, saying he wanted to defer supply.

The Goddess Strikes Back

"The government must go to the people," he said. "Let the people decide."

"Decide what? No one knows anything."

Brewer pressed his point. "If you don't side with us on this, the people might think you're hiding something – a mate of Clayton's, protecting a nest of traitors!"

"A nest of traitors? That's an old one, Ian. And how about you? Are you lily-white? What about your old mate Bono, not to mention the Company? This could be a CIA plot, for all we know!"

This slowed him up a bit.

"Oh, don't give me the old conspiracy theories, Mavis. And if the government's riddled with KGB officers, the CIA have every right to be interested."

We parted with the issue unresolved.

The whole thing gave me a very nasty feeling. I was worried about Bill. What had happened to him? Colette was depressed. Her Rome job was off. She and Virgil had recently split up, so it was a double whammy.

I had a meeting with Dandy Duckworth.

"We Independents had better stick together," I said. "What do you think about it all, Dandy?"

"I'm with you, Mavis."

"That's no help. I don't know where I am."

With friends like Dandy, I didn't need enemies.

My own position was very awkward. Being a friend of Bill's put me under a lot of pressure. Eventually, much against the grain, I agreed to side with Brewer in deferring supply – "until the situation was clarified". My friends in the government were not impressed.

The country was at a standstill.

Colette was upset about everything, and to get her mind off things I suggested a channelling session.

The following morning Matron rang me. "There's been a message from Cicero."

"Yes?"

"It says: 'Listen to tape'."

"Tape? Which one?"

"Perhaps he means Charles Tape."

"Matron, you're a genius."

Charles had decided to break precedent and go into the field himself.

I found him with his men in the safe house where Rakov was stashed away, up to his neck in files. He looked exhausted.

"Oh, hello, Mavis," he said.

Realising I wasn't going to go away, Charles resigned himself to a chat. He took me into an empty room.

"We've come across some very interesting documentation."

"Yes?"

"It confirms one of Rakov's wilder assertions."

"Oh?"

"It seems there might be a 'ring of three'."

"A ring of three?"

"Along the way, Bacchus seems to have recruited two friends to the cause – Apollo and Jupiter."

"Are you serious?"

"Deadly."

"Do we know their identities?"

"No, but they were known to Bacchus. He recruited them."

"Does the PM know?"

"Not yet. I'm on my way to tell him now. Rakov had some such story early in the piece, but he had no proof. I put it down to defector's dementia."

"Defector's dementia?"

"Defectors are a special breed, insecure, paranoid. And they have to have the goods. Sometimes they make things up to get people interested. Or they might become rattled and start imagining things. Either way, they're hard to handle. It's a big problem."

"And now we've got an even bigger problem – a ring of three. What is the collective noun for moles,

Charlie? A brace of moles? A pride of moles? A gaggle of moles?"

"I'll settle for a network."

"This complicates things. If one or two of the ring were in on the briefing, they could have alerted Clayton."

"They could have, or else there was an indiscretion by somebody, which led to them finding out."

"Could they have been in ASIO?"

"We can't rule out that possibility."

"The PM will be impressed – an ASIO man alerts Clayton and implicates the government, all in one shot."

"We don't know how Clayton was alerted, Mavis. And we don't know where Apollo and Jupiter are. That's the trouble."

"I'll leave you to it, Charles. Mum's the word. You'll have fun explaining to the Prime Minister why you didn't mention the ring of three at the beginning. Are the files authentic?"

"We're satisfied."

"What about Bill's coded message?"

"We're working on it. Just be patient."

"Charles, the country's falling apart. We've deferred supply. There are rallies every day. We need a breakthrough!"

The Goddess Strikes Back

The ring of three story came out. This disclosure heightened the paranoia and baying for blood. Lists of Bill's friends appeared; long lists. He seemed to have known everybody at one time or another. Investigative journalists were frantic. Find Apollo and Jupiter was the brief. No one was safe. The Cold War was over, but another war had started.

Somehow the government held on. But the money would soon run out. My vote and Dandy's were crucial. Were we doing the right thing? There were a few strange occurrences: reports of black rain falling in the outback. And Canberra suffered a huge blackout. It took three days to get the power back on. There was talk of a mystery virus spreading. A couple of MPs were seriously ill.

Then Colette got another message from Cicero: "Trouble brewing at Yarralumla".

I won't say how I smuggled myself into Government House, but it wasn't in a carpet or a crate of Bollinger. From behind a curtain I heard a very interesting conversation between Drover and Brewer. I peeped and saw Drover had a glazed look on his face. Brewer was in full flight.

"You've got no option. Sack them. They've got to go to the people. You don't owe Banks anything.

He axed you as leader, didn't he? They dumped you. Half of them are probably KGB. Be a statesman. I'll guarantee your job under my administration. You'll be a national hero!"

"You're probably right," Drover said.

"Oh, pull the other one!" I exploded, emerging from behind my camouflage.

I've never seen two more astonished faces.

"Pull yourself together, George," I said.

I turned to Brewer. "You think you're in the clear, don't you? Oh, I know you've been hobnobbing with the CIA for years. But you could be KGB yourself – you did business with Bill at one stage. You might be working for both sides – a double agent. Which one are you – Apollo or Jupiter? Or are you Janus, the two-faced god? Let's see that Roman profile!"

I jumped onto the couch and turned to Drover. "The government will have supply, George. I guarantee it."

I made my little discovery public. Brewer and Drover did their best to explain themselves but were no longer unsullied. The supply bills were passed, but a pall still hung over Australia. The Prime Minister looked older and tireder.

But Deirdre was having a great time. "I knew Clayton was no good. And I've never liked

The Goddess Strikes Back

Brewer, or Drover, or Banks. They're probably all KGB or CIA. Get all politicians and public servants into the Sydney Cricket Ground, line them up and say: 'Will anyone who isn't an agent please step forward'."

"At least you're developing a sense of humour."

"I'm serious."

"You'll break my heart one day, Deirdre."

Then late one afternoon a South Coast fisherman found a strange-looking shape washed up on the beach. It was a body: bloated, discoloured, with a bedraggled robe clinging to it. Kiama police were quick to act.

Our missing spy had come home.

19

Breaking the Code

I'd always thought it would be so civilised. Bill would turn up somewhere. There'd be a press conference. He'd tell us why he'd disappeared. He'd produce proof he wasn't a spy: it had all been a big mistake. Or, alternatively, he'd explain in his own urbane way, like Philby or Guy Burgess, why he had become a spy. And that'd be okay too. The Cold War was over anyway. Let the dead bury the dead. But Bill was dead. That was a fact. Who had buried him? Had he killed himself as some people had suggested? I felt we had only just started. Would we ever get to the bottom of it?

The discovery of Bill's body sobered us all

up. I was heartbroken. So was Colette. On the national stage, everyone became more serious. Banks was more sober. Brewer was less flamboyant. I knew Tape was more determined than ever to solve the mystery. As the days went by, Bacchus became the new cause. *Who killed Bacchus?* became the national question. Bill himself became popular. People wanted to know about him. A cult was developing. I was asked to do interviews.

"Why do spies always turn out to be more likeable than everybody else?" I asked Charles.

"They don't always," he replied. "It's a trick of the mind. Human psychology."

"I notice Rex Falcon wants to do a TV special canvassing the issues. We still don't know very much. I told him to bide his time," I said.

"Yes, even the post-mortem was inconclusive. They say Clayton may have been alive when he entered the water. There was no evidence of poisoning or force, except some abrasions on his lower right leg. It could have been suicide."

"In the meantime we've got the problem of Apollo and Jupiter. Don't the files give any clue to their positions or identities?"

"Unfortunately there are important gaps. Rakov's done his best, but he doesn't have all the documentation."

"What about Bill's coded message? It seems to be the only lead. Any more progress in cracking it?"

"We've tried everything. It's probably from a one-time code pad – that makes it unbreakable unless we find the corresponding pad. We found nothing in Clayton's house."

"Any other possibilities?"

"Some spies occasionally use book codes. These are codes based on a book known only to the sender and recipient. They're unbreakable unless you know the book."

"Maybe there's a clue somewhere else."

"We haven't found it."

"How's Rakov going?"

"Poor sod, he's worn out. He's going through our files, even closed ones. He's making a short list, or rather a long list, of people to follow up."

"You mean people who might be Apollo or Jupiter?"

"Yes, it's a long shot, but we're showing him files on everyone who's ever been regarded as a security risk, however minor, over the years. This is a serious situation. We've got to make progress."

"And Rakov will make a selection from these?"

"Yes."

"Who's on the list so far? Can you leak me

some names?"

Charles looked embarrassed.

"Come on Charles, give. I'm clean, you know that."

"Well, obviously Rakov's a bit over-zealous."

"Fire away."

"Okay. Try this list: Banks, Brewer, George Drover, Rex Falcon, you, Colette, Deirdre Dix, Dandy Duckworth, Brian Tooth, and some media people, senior ministers, public servants, academics, writers –"

"You had a file on all of us?"

"Most of them are closed. Don't worry."

"That's big of you. And what about ASIO people? Maybe some of you should be checked out?"

"Some of us are being checked out. We're being selective, there's nothing to worry about. Rakov's close to cracking up. He wants to feel useful. Oh, by the way, an old mate of yours is on the list – remember Vera Stone-Marten?"

"Vera? A mate? Never! If the tentacles of the KGB have penetrated that far, then we've all had it. Deirdre might be right, after all. You'll never be out of a job, Charles, not unless you're KGB yourself."

"I'll think about that one, Mavis."

With that we parted.

I went home depressed. Matron came out to meet me.

"Can you stand another message from Cicero?"

"I can always stand a message from Cicero."

"It's short and cryptic. There was a lot of interference. It's about the code."

"Okay. What is it?"

"Just three words: 'Conversation – Three – Manning'."

"'Conversation – Three – Manning'. Doesn't ring a bell. No further details?"

"I'm afraid not."

"Thanks anyway, Matron. I'll pass it on to Charles."

Charles was somewhat unimpressed, but said he'd work on it.

Two weeks later, Sydney University authorities were surprised to receive an official request that the third floor of Manning House be bugged and put under surveillance. ASIO had worked long and hard before getting to that point. They'd tried everything. Among other things, streets named Manning were investigated. Every house with a 3 Manning Street/Road address had been watched and bugged, but without success. Then a bright spark thought of Manning House. In desperation Charles agreed.

I liked the idea. Maybe there'd be a meeting, a sign, an indiscretion that would give a lead. Perhaps it would provide the final showdown: a confrontation between ASIO, Lark, and the moles; a chase across the campus; a defection on the footbridge crossing Parramatta Road, with a melancholy fade into the sunset of Forest Lodge.

But it wasn't to be. After two weeks of excruciating music from the bands outside, indifferent food, and endless student gossip, ASIO declared Manning to be PERSIL – thoroughly investigated and of no intelligence interest.

"Cicero's always come up with the goods in the past," I said to Charles.

"Yes, either transmission was bad, or he was being deliberately cryptic." Charles paused. "The most interesting one was the Tusculum Gallery. At least they saw a good exhibition."

"The Tusculum Gallery?"

"Yes. Three Manning Road, Potts Point – The Tusculum. John Verge's old villa refurbished, plus a gallery. Fascinating."

"Fascinating indeed...Conversation at the Tusculum, eh? But you didn't hear one?"

"Nothing relevant, no."

I thought for a minute. "Charles, may I have a

copy of Bill's coded message?"

"Of course. We made several copies for the cryptographers. I have one here."

"Thanks. I'll be in touch as soon as possible. I've got to do something first."

I rushed back to the office.

"Deirdre, where's that postcard?"

"What postcard?"

"The one we found in Bill's liquor cabinet."

Always efficient, she produced the card.

I read it again.

"Come on, Deirdre, we're going for a drive."

"Where to?"

"We're going to Bill's place again. I hope his relatives haven't cleaned him out."

The house seemed just the same. Quiet as a grave. Everything in place. ASIO had been careful. Even the book on the *Eleusinian Mysteries* had been shelved. Along one wall Bill had a series of nearly all the Penguin Classics, from Aesculus to Zola.

"Make us a drink, Deirdre," I said, tracing the shelves till I came to "C".

"C for Cicero," I said.

"I'll go along with that," she replied.

I murmured as I touched the volumes: "*Selected Political Speeches* – no; *Selected Works* – no;

Murder Trials – no; *On the Nature of the Gods* – no. Here we are, *On the Good Life*. I think this is the one. Let's see."

I looked at the contents page. "Yes, this is it."

I took the book to the coffee table, laid out the coded message and the postcard, and sat down. I opened the book and studied it for a minute.

"Have you ever read *Discussions at Tusculum*?" I asked.

"Never heard of it."

"It's one of Cicero's best works: a series of philosophical conversations set in his country villa at Tusculum, outside Rome."

"Okay. But what's all this got to do with Clayton?"

"I think Bill might have been using a book code."

"Why?" Deirdre asked, as she set the drinks on the table.

"Let's have a look at the postcard again."

I read it out loud: *"Dear Bill, greetings from Sydney. I changed plans and went to the Tusculum Gallery's latest exhibition. Had an interesting discussion with the curator. Hope life is being good to you. C."*

I continued: "Suppose the postcard is conveying something other than tourist chat. There are several possible keywords – for example, Tusculum, decision, life, good. There could be others, but let's take those. Then take Cicero's clue: 'Conversation – Three – Manning'. Three Manning Road, Potts Point, being the Tusculum. Conversation at the Tusculum, get it? It can't be a coincidence. Cicero's telling us something important, I'm sure of it, plus having a bit of fun at our expense. As soon as Charles told me about the Tusculum, I thought of the postcard and Bill's set of Penguin Classics."

I held up the book. "*Discussions at Tusculum* is included in *On the Good Life* – note the keywords. I think whoever wrote the postcard was telling Bill this is now the book for their coded communications. Deirdre, I'm hoping we can break the code. Let's have a drink before we start." We clinked our glasses. "Here's to the good life!"

"How does a book code work?" Deirdre asked, savouring her scotch.

"They vary, according to Charles. I'm going to try the most usual one first, with a slight variation."

I picked up the coded message. "As you can see, it's made up of sets of numbers, four numbers in a set. Let's take the first six sets: 1-2-7-12 1-2-4-6 1-2-8-5 1-2-5-3 1-2-3-2 1-2-7-7. Let's say each set of numbers represents a letter. Notice the first two numbers in each set are the same – namely one and two. I think these two numbers identify the page of the book, the third number the line on the page, and the fourth number the place of the letter on the line – first, second, twentieth, whatever."

Deirdre was riveted. "Why are there two separate numbers to identify the page?"

"Good question, my dear Watson."

I opened the book at *Discussions at Tusculum*, and showed her. "See, there are two numbers at the top of each page. They represent the section numbering of the original text. I think the writer of the message used these to identify the page, and he used the same page to make it easy."

"I get it."

"Let's try it out. Now for the first set: 1-2-7-12. So, we're on the page numbered 1-2. Let's assume the next number, 7, represents the seventh line on that page, and the fourth number, 12, represents the twelfth letter on that line. Now, let's count down and across…We get 'U' as our first letter. Okay. So let's try the second set: 1-2-4-6. Same page, fourth line, sixth letter…we get 'R' as our second letter. The third set: 1-2-8-5. Same page, eighth line, fifth letter…we get 'G' as our third letter."

On the same reasoning the fourth letter was

"E"…the fifth letter, "N". My excitement was mounting. The sixth letter was "T". U-R-G-E-N-T.

"Urgent. Could that be by chance, Deirdre? I doubt it. I think we're on to something."

By the same process, the full message unravelled in all its glory: *"Urgent You have been blown Use countersurveillance measures Must meet re contingency plans Mrs Macquarie's Chair four am November first L"*.

We sat in silence for a minute.

"No doubt L stands for Lark," I said, "Bill's controller. Rakov says Lark controls all three – Bacchus, Apollo, and Jupiter. The postcard was telling Bill the book for coded messages had changed. They probably changed the book regularly. Bill had nearly all the Penguin Classics. Lark or Moscow could use any one as long as they let Bill know. The message by postcard was probably a regular thing, like a game between him and Lark. You know how playful Bill was. And for some reason he kept his last one. He must have got rid of everything else incriminating. ASIO found nothing but the coded message."

"And notice the meeting date – 4 a.m., November first. The day after Halloween," Deidre said.

"Yes, he probably went to the rendezvous straight from the party, still in fancy dress – as

The Goddess Strikes Back

Queen Hatshepsut. It was a very good anti-surveillance tactic, and it worked."

"But it didn't save his life."

"No, that's the big gap in the story. He went to meet his controller at Mrs Macquarie's Chair. What happened then? He must have wondered what the 'contingency plans' would be. He was in such a vulnerable position. He knew so much. He knew the identity of Apollo and Jupiter. But the Cold War was over. Would Moscow want him? Would he want to go there anyway? What were Lark's instructions, and did he follow them? Everything was a game to Bill. Maybe spying was as well. Perhaps he was sick of the game. He may have intended to talk and blow everybody."

"And Lark knew that."

"Possibly. Well, Deirdre, I think it's time we let Charles in on the secret."

20

The Gold Beetle

Charles was jubilant.

"Brilliant, Mavis," he said. "Of course, if we'd had the postcard…"

"Life's full of ifs, Charlie."

"Clayton was in fancy dress when his body was found, so he might have gone straight to the rendezvous from the party, and from there to his death."

"He might have left the rendezvous by boat. Mrs Macquarie's Chair is right on Woolloomooloo Bay."

"Good point."

"Charles, what contingency plans would you expect Bill to be given?"

"Moscow wouldn't want old blown spies. He'd probably be told to weather the storm and keep his mouth shut. At best to confess himself, but keep the others out of it. The game has changed, but every country needs spies, particularly in the economic area. Clayton knew Apollo and Jupiter. He recruited them. Very insecure, but that's the way it was. We don't know whether Apollo and Jupiter knew about each other, but Lark controlled them all. According to Rakov, Lark's probably been here for years comfortably established in some cover or other. Very likely he wouldn't want to return to Moscow, even if he were recalled. Look at Rakov – he didn't want to stay in the system. A crumbling empire. No use to an old school KGB officer, or an agent used to the good life. Life's comfortable here. Better the capitalism you know than the capitalism you don't."

"Bill had become a bit expendable, hadn't he? The weak link. He could have blown them all sky high to save himself. And Rakov had more than they realised. So what now, Charles?"

"We'll re-interview the party guests, and go over the rendezvous site thoroughly. Maybe something will show up."

"May I come?"

"I wouldn't be without you."

So the operation started. A contingent of top-level ASIO officers, police, and the forensic squad proceeded down Art Gallery Road, into Mrs Macquaries Road to the target area.

Charles and I decided to go on foot, possibly the way Bill had himself arrived at the rendezvous. So we walked, past the art gallery, past the Pavilion Restaurant, past the National Herbarium, past Henry Lawson's statue, past the lawns and Moreton Bay figs. Everything beautifully kept. Nothing out of place. We talked as we walked.

"Bill probably came here on foot," I said. "He knew he'd beaten the watchers. He might have got a cab to the top of Art Gallery Road and walked the rest of the way."

"I wonder how Lark came, and who got there first."

"And what happened then?"

Eventually we arrived at the chair. Charles conferred with his men and the police. They'd found nothing so far, but were still combing the area.

One of the men said: "The trouble is, it being a well-kept tourist spot, any evidence there was is probably gone."

"Maybe," Charles replied.

Charles and I walked down the stairway to the chair itself.

The Goddess Strikes Back

"Let's go and sit on the chair," I said.

It was surprisingly comfortable. We gazed out on the water.

"I can see why Mrs Macquarie liked to sit here," I said. "It's so peaceful. You could forget you were in a colonial outpost."

Charles brought me back to earth. "Clayton and Lark might have sat here as they talked," he said.

I surveyed the stone around us, the stairs, the ceiling. "No sign chiselled into the rock, no chalk mark, no skull and crossbones."

Charles rose abruptly. "Let's keep walking," he said.

We took the lower pathway skirting Woolloomooloo Bay.

"Perfect getaway point if you had a boat," he said.

After a few minutes we walked back towards the chair and approached the stairway. One of the men came rushing down to meet us.

"We've found something, sir."

He handed Charles a tiny object.

"Found it wedged in the ring of a cut branch. It was almost invisible. Only saw it because it caught the sunlight."

Charles examined the object.

"A gold beetle, with a pin attached – an earring."

"A scarab!" I exclaimed. "May I see?"

He showed me the earring.

"I bet it belonged to Bill," I said. "He had a whole collection of ancient Egyptian scarabs. He had some reworked into jewellery – rings, broaches, bracelets, earrings. It's a symbol of renewed life."

"Not very appropriate in his case," Charles observed. "Let's see the tree."

We bounded up the stairs and the men directed us to the relevant Moreton Bay fig.

"It was a signal, but to whom?" Charles said, examining the branch that was just above head height. "The miracle is that no one has snatched it before now. You found nothing else in the tree?"

"No sir."

"What about the inside?" I asked. "The hole at the base is huge. You could nearly fit a body in there."

"We searched, Mavis. Only stones, sticks, and dead leaves."

"Mind if I have a look?"

"Go ahead."

I entered the tree at the base and dug around. Nothing. I went a bit deeper, deeper, and hit something. It felt like glass. I dug for the object and uncovered a green bottle. I emerged and examined the find: an empty half-bottle of Moet and Chandon Brut Imperial. Inside it was a rolled up sheet of paper.

"Gentlemen, I think we are on to something." I held up the bottle. "Bill's favourite brand!"

"What's that inside it?" somebody asked.

"Not the *Young Endeavour*, I hope," another man quipped.

"No, better still – a message," I flashed back.

I handed Charles the bottle. "Would you do the honours, please?"

He was glad to oblige. He borrowed a skewer-like instrument from one of the forensic squad and tried to extract the scroll, but without success. The bottle had to be broken.

Charles unfurled the paper and read it aloud: *"M and friends, suspect an ambush. If I disappear, find the others. H may help. B."*

"Starkly simple," Charles said. "But it confirms our brief. I am sure 'M' refers to you, Mavis. There are others, and we'll find them."

"What about 'H'?" one of the men asked.

"We'll have to think about that," Charles replied.

A few days later, in the Prime Minister's office, the three of us took stock.

"It's hard to pick Bill's motivation exactly," I said. "Leaving the postcard and the coded message in his house suggests either he didn't care anymore, or that he actively wanted people to put two and two together. He might have suspected the rendezvous from the start."

"But he abided by the conditions," the Prime Minister said. "He took anti-surveillance measures and kept the appointment."

"What choice would he have?" Charles said. "He had nowhere to go, really. The game was up."

"And to cap it off, he left the message at the chair," I said.

"I wonder how he got the scarab earring?" the PM said.

"It belonged to his lady friend – a gift from Clayton years ago. She was an old flame, apparently," Charles replied.

"And the champagne bottle he could have got easily at the party," I said. "It seems as though he made the decision to leave a message while he was at the party, as though something there had made him suspicious of the plans Lark had in store…What did he mean by 'ambush'? Did he really suspect his life was in danger?"

"Not necessarily. He might have thought he'd be forced underground, or forced to do something he didn't want to do, like retiring to Moscow. But he wasn't prepared to carry the can alone."

"If only he'd given us more information in the message."

"Too risky," Charles replied. "He couldn't have known for sure what would happen. It was his own contingency plan. He might have wanted to retrieve it later. If the message giving incriminating details was found by the wrong people before he got to it, he'd be in strife. But at least the message confirms the existence of the others."

"What about the reference to 'H'?" the PM asked.

"The only 'H' I can think of is Hatshepsut," Charles said. "The queen he impersonated at the party."

"She's been dead for three thousand years, so it doesn't sound like a very fruitful line of enquiry," the PM snapped.

"Granted," Charles replied.

"What about the lady friend at the party?"

"We're certain she knows nothing."

"So where do we go from here?" the PM asked.

"We are going all-out. The police are working at full capacity. The party guests have drawn a blank, but a taxi driver remembers someone answering Clayton's description getting out near

St Mary's Cathedral around three a.m. on that morning. We are also looking at the boat angle. So far no one has come forward with information about a boat in Woolloomooloo Bay. The Maritime Services Board have been willing, but haven't been able to help. We haven't found any eyewitnesses en route to the chair or at the chair."

"It sounds like a long haul," the PM said. "The British and Americans are on our backs. We've got to clean up our act, we're an international laughing stock."

"But everybody's forgotten about the recession," I said.

"We'll have to follow up on Rakov's list and start questioning people."

"And Cicero's not available," I said. "Colette tells me he's on holidays."

"He's picked a lousy time to cop out," the PM growled.

"We've had a pretty good run," I replied.

With that, Charles and I left the PM and walked back to my office. I invited him in for a drink.

When we were settled, Charles cleared his throat.

"Mavis, I've been thinking about Hatshepsut."
"Oh?"

"I wonder if Bill was referring to her?"

"Hard to say," I replied.

"I don't want to intrude, but I've been talking to Matron and Colette..."

"Yes?"

"I understand you have...a relationship...involving time travel or some such. It's a long shot, but I wondered if Hatshepsut herself may know something?"

I stopped short. "I hadn't thought of that. Back to Hat again, eh?"

"We've got to explore all avenues. Bill meant something by 'H', perhaps he meant Hatshepsut."

"Perhaps. He did know about my trips, that's true."

Charles sighed. "There are more things in heaven and earth –"

"Yes, Charles, yes."

"Remember, Bill addressed his message to you: 'M and friends'. It's a sacred trust really, isn't it?"

"All right Charlie, don't overdo it. I'll think about it."

21

The Final Stretch

I hadn't been back to see Hat for ages but Colette and Matron were enthusiastic.

"Go back, darling," Colette said. "Hat has always helped you when you needed it."

After a few pinot noirs I was off. Hat's lady-in-waiting was there to greet me.

"They're at the pictures, Mavis," she said. "Give them another five minutes."

Soon after, Hat emerged looking upset. Sen had his arm around her.

"Darling, it was only a movie," he said.

"Oh, it was so unnecessary," she said.

They crossed the atrium and saw me.

"Mavis! What are you doing here?"

"I need your help."

"Let's go to our apartments, where we can talk in peace," Sen said.

When we got to the apartment Sen helped Hat to a chair and poured us each a beer.

"Cheers! What was the film?" I asked.

Sen replied. "It was a spy night – a double bill. Burgess and Maclean were the first half... fascinating. And the second half was your little story in Australia –"

"*Bacchus: The Final Days*," Hat interrupted.

"Great title. Tell me about it," I said.

"You probably know it all already."

"No I don't, that's the trouble."

Hat was still agitated. "Poor Bill, all dressed up and where did he go? To an ambush. It was so calculated and heartless. But the party was terrific. The costume was fabulous. I wonder where she got the material?"

"Tell Mavis the story," Sen said.

"I knew that pirate at the party was no good –"

"Pirate?"

"A man dressed up as...who was it, darling?... Captain Kidd, that's right. Watching Bill all night out of the corner of his eye."

"Was he ASIO?" I asked.

"ASIO? The fools in the car outside! No, they couldn't find their way out of a department store. Bill was a wake-up to ASIO, that's why he changed costume. No, Captain Kidd was a KGB watcher working for Lark. But Bill recognised him – that was Lark's mistake."

"Hat, I think we should take it from the beginning," Sen said.

"Better still, can we have a rerun?" I asked.

So we headed back to the cinema. The projectionist was called back and put on double time.

Bacchus: The Final Days was a grainy, 1950s-look documentary in black and white, with an FBI style voice-over. We saw it all. Rakov's defection through to Tape's briefing of the Prime Minister and the Security Committee. Then the bit I didn't know – Lark being signalled by phone for an urgent communication. Lark picks up a message from a post office box. Lark contacts Moscow. Moscow replies – Clayton is to deny everything. Keep the others in place, if possible. Then Lark's meeting with Apollo in the early hours of the morning. Lark fully visible. Apollo shrouded in darkness, a disembodied voice talking softly. I listened to that voice, recognised it, and froze.

A similar meeting with Jupiter: another voice in the darkness, another voice I recognised.

The Goddess Strikes Back

The same softly spoken conversation. The same agreement reached. "He's unreliable...always said he'd talk if he got caught...too much at stake...he's blown and clapped-out...he's no use...too risky...Moscow doesn't understand... I'm valuable where I am... why risk my career?" Lark agrees to see to it.

Lark has the coded message delivered to Bill's desk by hand, in an envelope of art catalogues. This is a change from the usual signal for meetings. He also arranges for Bill to be discreetly watched. Lark isn't certain Bill will keep the appointment. He doesn't want Bill to disappear before he gets to him.

We see Bill decoding the message at home in the bathroom. After decoding, he screws up the sheet and throws it on the floor. He clears up and destroys all other evidence. He doesn't touch the liquor cabinet. He travels to his Sydney house and cleans up. He goes to the Halloween party as Cicero. ASIO waits outside. We see the KGB watcher, disguised as Captain Kidd, circulating and watching Bill. Bill recognises him.

Cicero meets Queen Hatshepsut, an old flame. They get together and change costume, including wig, gown, scarab earrings, and handbag. The party wears on. Bill writes his message and searches for an empty bottle and torch. He leaves the party quickly and quietly, unrecognised by ASIO. He gets a cab in New South Head Road. Captain Kidd follows in his own car. Bill gets out at St Mary's Cathedral. Captain Kidd parks and watches. Bill proceeds down Art Gallery Road. Captain Kidd rings Lark from a payphone near St James Station confirming Bill is proceeding to the rendezvous.

Bill proceeds to Mrs Macquarie's Chair. He hasn't been followed. No one is around. Everything is clear. He looks surreal: an Egyptian queen in black and white silhouette moving in the dimly lit area. It is well before sunrise. He selects the tree, places the scarab, buries the bottle, and waits, sitting on the chair overlooking the water. Everything is silent.

Meanwhile, Tony Sharp, alias Lark, successful art dealer and man about town, boards his luxury launch moored at his Kirribilli residence. He proceeds to Woolloomooloo Bay. Sharp anchors, disembarks, and walks to the chair. He joins Bill and they talk. Sharp tells Bill a high-level plan is being devised to discredit Rakov and the whole thing as a sham. ASIO won't have a leg to stand on. He's taking Bill to a safe house at Watsons Bay where he'll be fully briefed. He assures Bill everything will be okay. Bill hesitates and turns slightly, as if thinking of something, perhaps the message in the tree. Then he agrees.

Bill and Sharp walk to the launch. They set off. Sharp offers Bill a swig of brandy from a flask. Bill accepts. Shortly afterwards Bill blacks out. Sharp stops the launch, checks that Bill is well and truly unconscious, and proceeds to bind a heavy stone to his right ankle with wire. He starts up again and soon is going through the Heads. Out at sea, still before sunrise, Bill is heaved overboard. He sinks without trace. Sharp returns to Kirribilli.

The rest I knew.

At the end the voice-over tells us investigations are continuing.

We sat in silence.

"Is it what you wanted, Mavis?" Hat asked.

"Yes and no," I replied wearily.

"We didn't actually see Apollo and Jupiter. Did you recognise the voices?" Sen asked.

"Unfortunately, yes."

"You were always good at voices," Hat said.

"You look as depressed as Hat was," Sen said. "It's only a film, remember?"

"Tell that to Bill," I replied. Then I brightened up. "But thanks to you both, it's been a big help."

"What are you going to do now?" Sen asked.

"I'm not sure. I'll go back to Sydney, sleep on it, then talk to Charles."

"Would the film help?"

"That's an idea. May I take it with me?"

"Sure. We've seen it twice now."

I had a drink for the road and headed home.

22

The Sting

Matron and Colette were waiting for me.

"How was it?"

"Informative," I replied. "I think I'll go to bed. We'll talk about it in the morning."

Next day, after giving them a censored version of the trip, I had a conference with Charles. He was riveted by the film, but agreed it mightn't be admissible evidence. Just as I had been, he was floored by the voices on the soundtrack.

Speaking of the murder, he said: "The brandy obviously contained a potent drug of some kind, but it didn't show up in the post-mortem. I'm not surprised – KGB laboratories researched drugs and poisons for years. They had it down to a fine art. In any case, Sharp wasn't expecting the body to show up, having weighted it with a rock. That's the part that intrigues me – the wire didn't hold."

"Lots of things can happen under the sea," I said. "And Bacchus is always looked after."

"Not quite well enough, though."

"It's not over yet."

"No, it's not. Knowing Lark's identity is a huge breakthrough. That might take us all the way if we play our cards right."

"What about Captain Kidd?"

"We'll see what we can find. In the meantime say nothing, keep cool, act normally, and we'll see what develops."

Lots of my friends wanted to know where I'd been.

"Just a short holiday," I'd say. "All this spy hunting is tiring."

Apart from Colette and Matron only Charles had known about my real destination.

The Prime Minister was pleased to see me. "I feel better when you're around," he said.

"Any news on the spy front?" I asked.

"No, I haven't seen Tape for a week. I have a feeling the issue will go off the boil if nothing happens. People are more interested in the recession, anyway."

"Maybe."

Brewer was his usual self – energetic and keen to clean things up.

I dropped in on Foreign Affairs.

"Found any more spies?" the minister asked.

"No Minister, but I'll keep you posted."

George Drover rang and asked me over to dinner at Yarralumla. I accepted.

"No hard feelings," he said, referring to my surprise appearance from behind the curtain and its aftermath.

"No probs, George," I said.

Brian Tooth was still serious. "There's more to come, I'm sure of it," he said.

"Maybe," I replied.

And Rex Falcon paid me a visit.

"Glad you left office?" I asked him.

"I don't envy Banks at the moment," he replied. "And show business has its compensations."

A few days later, Charles came to see me. He looked devastated.

"Tony Sharp was killed in a car accident yesterday."

"That's interesting. Maybe there is a God."

"That's not my concern, Mavis. This means our key player has gone. He was under round-the-clock surveillance. Sooner or later something may have shown up."

"Do you suspect foul play?"

"No. He skidded on wet road and hit another car. Both Sharp and the other driver were killed instantly."

"Have you searched his premises?"

"Yes. We found the usual stuff – transmitter, cameras, code-pads, a copy of *The Good Life*, some documentation."

"But nothing on Apollo and Jupiter?"

"No."

"Have you found anything on Captain Kidd?"

"Rakov saw part of the film and recognised him. He's an old KGB courier from way back. Very loyal; did what he was told. We doubt that he knew of the murder plan. Lark probably used him occasionally over the years."

"Another dead end," I said. "Why don't we sleep on it? I'll see you in the morning."

At nine o'clock sharp, I was on his doorstep. My mind was buzzing.

"Charles, I think we should publicise the death of such a successful and talented art dealer."

"You mean make sure Apollo and Jupiter know their controller is dead? They probably know already from Moscow, but let's make sure. Sharp was well known. They must have known his cover identity."

Charles continued: "And Moscow will be keeping well out of it. I doubt they'll be sending in a replacement just yet. So what are you up to?"

"I've been thinking. There just may be a way of solving our problem. It's tricky, but I think we could make it work. Let's go for a walk. We don't want to be overheard…"

During the next week a few articles appeared in the newspapers about Tony Sharp, art dealer and businessman extraordinaire. His loss was mourned by collectors, curators, academics, showbiz people, politicians. Everyone knew about the tragic death of Tony Sharp.

"What a high profile he had!" I said to Deirdre.

"A capitalist pig!" she retorted.

Life went on. After a chat with me, Rex Falcon decided it was time to have a serious in-depth program on the Cold War and its aftermath, with the main emphasis on espionage. The program, to be entitled *The Cold War: A Post-mortem*, would be a high-flying, high-budget enterprise, with top guests from Australia and overseas. The guest list would include the PM, Brewer, the Minister for Foreign Affairs, Charles Tape and former ASIO chiefs, senior politicians from both sides of politics, Foreign Affairs people, diplomats, Brian Tooth and other journalists, and of course, myself.

Even George Drover, the Governor General, an ex-Foreign Minister himself was persuaded to attend.

The program would be telecast live to air, with a studio audience of the general public. Features would include satellite interviews with British and American espionage experts, plus selected footage of Cold War highlights, including the Burgess and Maclean story, the Petrov affair, the Rosenberg case, and the famous 1954 press conference where Philby protests his innocence standing by the fireplace in his mother's living room. Rex was having a ball getting it all together. Rakov was to be a guest, along with another elderly defector, now residing in Australia, who had known Theodore Maly and Arnold Deutsch, two famous controllers of the Cambridge Five.

And behind the scenes, Charles and I were oiling our own machinery.

Deirdre asked me to get her a seat in the general public section.

"Okay," I said. "But take your knitting, in case you get bored."

And so the day came. Rex welcomed everybody. Guests were organised. Bodyguards and security paraphernalia had to be attended to. Rex was to sit at the centre of proceedings at a large current affairs-style desk, complete with phone.

The Goddess Strikes Back

"Will the phone ring, Rex?" someone asked.

"I hope so," he replied.

Guests were to be seated on both sides of Rex. There was a bit of shuffling and joking about who should be to the right or left of the desk. But eventually things were sorted out. There were two screens in the studio: one for film clips and one for satellite interviews. General public seating had been booked out for weeks. We had a very full house.

And so *The Cold War: A Post-mortem* went live to air. Rex made an introductory statement encapsulating the history of the decades since World War II, and ended by asking: "Where do we go to now? What about espionage? What is its role now?"

Various guests said their piece: the Prime Minister, the Minister for Foreign Affairs, Charles Tape and former ASIO chiefs, Brewer, Drover, Brian Tooth. Yuri Dominov, the man who'd known Maly and Deutsch, was an eager participant. Then followed some historic film clips and satellite interviews with British and American experts.

How the game had changed! The KGB was now the Federal Security Service of the Russian Federation. The ideological spy was dead. Defection was no longer an industry. Defence was no longer the big issue. Economics was the new game. Spies, we need, but in a different area.

"Where will the new spies be?" asked a member of the audience.

"In the Treasury and Reserve Bank, probably," said one expert.

"What about agents still in place?"

"Moscow can't afford to withdraw all its spies worldwide. They'll let some sleep. Others they'll redeploy."

"What about Apollo and Jupiter?" asked someone else.

"Good question," Rex said.

"We are working on it," Charles said.

"Will Moscow leave them in place?"

Both Rakov and Dominov thought they would.

"What about their controller, Lark?"

Dominov spoke. "Him too. Long-term agents with a good cover could still be invaluable."

Dominov was a charismatic man who seemed to invite conversation. He was questioned about controllers and their function.

"They keep up morale, encourage, advise, and look after things generally."

He reminisced about the old days in Europe and told how Maly and Deutsch had been heroes, with portraits hanging in the KGB Memory Room.

"Controllers are vitally important. I know, I was one myself."

A wit from the audience piped up: "Maybe you still are."

Dominov laughed.

The man persisted. "Maybe you're Lark, holding the hands of Apollo and Jupiter."

Dominov remained jovial. "I'm sure Lark is a good agent. But I assure you I've retired from the game."

Then Rex's phone rang.

Rex lifted the receiver, listened for a minute, then laughed.

He spoke to the audience. "It's Lark!" he exclaimed.

He listened again, then still smiling, addressed Ian Brewer.

"He wants to talk to you, Ian. He's got some information."

Brewer seemed surprised, but adjusted quickly. Obviously prepared to go along with a joke, he rose to his feet and walked to the phone. He picked up the receiver with a theatrical gesture.

"Hullo, is that you, Lark? I wish you'd spill the beans and clean up this mess about Apollo and Jupiter!"

He stopped and listened. In seconds he was transformed. His face went grey. His whole body crumpled. He stumbled. His eyes stared.

He looked towards Rex Falcon.

"What's wrong, Ian?" Rex asked.

"What are you playing at?" Brewer croaked.

"Who is it?" Falcon asked. "Who's on the phone?"

The studio was completely silent.

"I'll tell you who it is," Falcon continued. "It's Bill Clayton, our spy, Bacchus."

Brewer couldn't answer.

A low buzz went around the studio.

"Bill…it's Bill…Bill Clayton…Bacchus…"

I looked towards the Prime Minister. The expression on his face was interesting, and Australia saw it. He rose to his feet.

"What are you trying to pull, Rex?" he snarled.

"Wait and see," Rex replied.

Doors opened. Matron entered, wheeling a chair. In the chair was Colette, eyes closed, in full channelling mode. Having done her bit on the phone, she was ready for the second act.

Rex took the floor and addressed the camera.

"Men and women of Australia, I am honoured to present to you Colette, channeller extraordinaire and national treasure. Through Colette we are happy to invite into the living rooms of Australia, Mr Bill Clayton, alias Bacchus."

There was applause.

"Hullo everyone, it's a pleasure to be here." Bill's voice was unmistakable, unforgettable. The urbane drawl I knew so well.

Colette was oblivious, but Matron stood firmly behind her. At a signal from Rex I joined Matron behind the chair.

Rex continued: "Colette and Bill have kindly offered their services to Australia in a very special broadcast."

Charles stepped forward. "Hullo, Bill. Thanks for joining us. It's Charles Tape here, the head of ASIO."

"Hullo, Charles," Bill replied.

"I know you can't see, but you can hear, is that right?" Charles asked.

"I can hear perfectly," Bill said.

"That's excellent. Bill, we've got a bit of Cold War footage here, and we were hoping you could fill us in on one or two points."

"I'd be delighted," Bill replied.

The studio darkened, the eyes of Australia went to the empty screen and *Bacchus: The Final Days* went to air.

Epilogue

The Greeks used to talk about catharsis, a cleansing. Certainly we were cleansed of Banks and Brewer, Apollo and Jupiter. A profound shock to the nation but we survived. Some found help by going back to the ancient Greco-Roman mystery cults. Egyptology became popular too.

The biggest plus for Colette and me was the revival of interest in the classics. All over Australia students were queueing up to gain admission to Classics departments. Latin was all the rage and Cicero top of the pops.

"He's really made a comeback," someone said.

"He never left," Colette snapped.

The Goddess Strikes Back

Of course, in the real world it's business as usual. Banks and Brewer were replaced. Apollo and Jupiter were just as surprised about each other as Australia was about them. The players and cards are reshuffled, and the game goes on.

I'll continue on in parliament for the time being. Colette wants to go for a trip. You know – Rome, Cairo, Alexandria, all that. I may join her.

Sometimes, when we're in the Sydney office, Colette, Matron and I take a bottle or two and go down to Mrs Macquarie's Chair. We drink a toast, gaze out on the water, and dream our dreams. I often think of the good old days in Egypt.

Acknowledgements

I would like to thank John Clarke, Jim McClelland, and Rosemary Creswell for their encouragement.

Thanks also to my editor, Glenda Downing.

www.ingramcontent.com/pod-product-compliance
Lightning Source LLC
Chambersburg PA
CBHW021103080526
44587CB00010B/363